# Art Auctions

# Hot Topics in the Art World

Published in association with Sotheby's Institute of Art

## Series Editors

Jeffrey Boloten and Juliet Hacking, Sotheby's Institute of Art, London

This series of short, thought-provoking and sometimes controversial books debates key issues of current relevance to art-world professionals working in both the private and public sectors. The texts give wider visibility to some critical areas of professional art-world practice, considering what disruptors are challenging the status quo and how the art world is likely to be transformed over the next decades as a result.

## International Series Advisory Board

# Art Auctions

## Spectacle and Value in the 21st Century

Kathryn Brown

LUND HUMPHRIES

Sotheby's INSTITUTE OF ART

First published in 2024 by Lund Humphries
in association with Sotheby's Institute of Art

Lund Humphries
Huckletree Shoreditch
Alphabeta Building
18 Finsbury Square
London EC2A 1AH
UK
www.lundhumphries.com



ISBN (hardback): 978-1-84822-638-8
ISBN (eBook PDF): 978-1-84822-643-2
ISBN (eBook ePub): 978-1-84822-642-5

A Cataloguing-in-Publication record for this book is available from the British Library



Copy edited by Michela Parkin
Designed by Crow Books
Set in Caslon Pro and Sofia Pro
Printed in Estonia

# Contents

# Foreword

Art auctions occupy a highly prominent place in the art world, and in the public perception of that world, owing to the extraordinary prices and the intense excitement that they generate. As auction-price data is publicly accessible (whereas that pertaining to commercial galleries is not), it is conventional to derive all art-market data and analysis from auction results. The theatrical nature of art auctions, with their distinctive rules and choreography, appears charmingly out of step with modern business practices. Indeed, the standard model for auctioning items of artistic value has, until recently, hardly changed since the mid-18th century when Sotheby's and Christie's were first established.

In recent years, with the rapid and extensive financialisation of the art world, the acquisition of auction houses by large conglomerates seeking to monetise the model, and the threat to viability posed by the COVID-19 pandemic, auction houses have emerged as significant art-world innovators. The multi-national auction houses have, for example, capitalised on emergent digital technologies to create online multi-site auctions, to trade in digital art and to accept bids in cryptocurrencies. In this new and original study, Kathryn Brown astutely and engagingly traces the origins of the distinctive performance that is the art auction, examines the symbolic (and therefore economic) value attached to them and to the artworks on sale, and argues that the most recent incarnations of this legacy business model are as much about spectacle – and the value we attach to spectacle – as ever.

*Jeffrey Boloten and Juliet Hacking, February 2024*

# Acknowledgements

Over the course of writing this book, I have benefitted from conversations about auctions and art commerce with numerous friends and colleagues. I am grateful, in particular, to Dirk Boll, Simon de Pury, D'Lan Davidson and Philip Dodd for generously sharing their experiences at the cutting edge of the contemporary art auction business and commercial gallery landscape. Frances Fowle, Alain Quemin and Georgina Walker have been important conversation partners about art markets over several years. Ideas from chapters have been presented at events hosted by Edinburgh University, the University of Melbourne, Loughborough University, the University of York, the Musée de Grenoble and the Royal Academy of Arts, London. Participants in those events have encouraged me to probe further the possibilities and risks that arise from the increasing merger of cultural and financial landscapes. Alan Thomas has, as ever, provided invaluable advice and encouragement throughout the writing journey. I would also like to thank Juliet Hacking and Jeffrey Boloten for supporting the idea for the book and for their comments on the text. Keen editorial input from Lucy Myers at Lund Humphries has been vital to the publication process.

# Introduction

Auctions stage powerful dramas about the different values that are ascribed to artworks. On the one hand, the outcome of a competitive bidding process imposes temporary clarity on the financial worth of artefacts that are typically difficult to price.[1] On the other hand, the extent to which an artwork's price tag corresponds to its aesthetic, historical and social importance is something that has been, and continues to be, a subject of contention. By tracing the changing spectacle of art auctions, this book explores the ongoing relevance of this public sales format to contemporary art markets and discusses important opportunities, controversies and conflicts of value to which it gives rise.

When a painting titled *Peinture-poème (Musique, Seine, Michel, Bataille et moi)* by Surrealist artist Joan Miró failed to meet its reserve price at a Christie's auction in 2022, it was later acquired by the Museum Boijmans Van Beuningen, Rotterdam, in a private sale for approximately US$8.3 million.[2] Post-auction sales are often a corrective to high estimates (sometimes demanded by the seller), and unsold works are graphically referred to as 'burned' on the market. The museum managed to acquire Miró's painting at the lower end of the auction house estimate. If public failure in the market did not impinge on the museum's estimation of the work's cultural significance, what does this tell us about the supposed consensus on value achieved in the auction arena? Which factors take precedence in determining the broader cultural merits of an artwork: institutional recognition, expert opinion or market success? Auctions are the most visible arena of clashes between these competing ideas about value, and their dramas have long-term consequences for artists, collectors, gallerists, museums and publics.

## A Hot Topic

If auctions are a familiar part of the art landscape, what makes them a 'hot topic' today? The first reason concerns the visibility of their action and outcomes. Auctions generate eye-catching spectacle in their physical set-up, bidding rivalries, auctioneer performances and creation of legend. Applause frequently breaks out when a work is knocked down at a record-breaking price. Describing the 2017 Christie's sale of *Salvator Mundi* attributed to Leonardo da Vinci for US$450.3 million, art journalist Scott Reyburn recalls that the audience 'gasped and whooped as if they'd just seen a rocket explode high above their heads'.[3]

Whereas the prices at which artworks change hands in private sales remain undisclosed, the results of auctions are public (with the exception of certain details regarding fees and guarantees) and are widely covered in the press. In consequence, these events produce a wealth of financial information about art and artists that is often used as a barometer for gauging the condition of the art market as a whole. Although the methodologies for data collection are often inconsistent, the hunger for pricing information among collectors and gallerists is voracious. This has seen the rise of a data industry specialised in the gathering and analysis of auction estimates, results and trends.

According to one such business, Artprice, the global turnover in the fine art auction market in 2022 was US$16.5 billion (the fourth-highest year in history).[4] Within that headline figure, large auction houses achieved some eye-catching returns across a range of striking events.

Phillips boasted a 'white glove' auction (a sale in which all lots are sold) of works by David Hockney in September 2022 and followed this with another sale dedicated entirely to the artist's output in 2023.[5] Christie's auctions of works by noted collectors including the late Paul G. Allen (co-founder of Microsoft), the French fashion designer Hubert de Givenchy and the Swiss gallerists Thomas and Doris Ammann broke records for the prices achieved by individual lots and, in the case of the Allen sale, for an art auction itself (over US$1.5 billion).[6] In November 2023, Sotheby's sale of works from the collection of the late Whitney Museum patron, Emily Fisher Landau, became the highest grossing auction sale dedicated to a female collector (US$406.4 million).[7]

Events such as these generate market spectacle in their own right, but they also highlight a second theme that attests to the 'hotness' of auctions: power. Sociologists Luc Boltanski and Arnaud Esquerre argue that international auction businesses have attained unprecedented levels of influence in the 21st century and that they fashion a global art market 'unified from above'.[8] By encouraging the public's focus on international market trends, record-breaking prices, celebrity artists and ultra-high-net-worth collectors, activities at the top end of the market mirror, and arguably reinforce, broader inequalities of wealth and income within and across nations. In Boltanski and Esquerre's view, the result is a cultural environment that contrasts 'a very small number of ultra-beneficiaries – the stars – with a very large number of rejects'.[9] This means that the auction industry is capable of encouraging a 'winner-take-all' market in which rewards go to artists with the strongest brands, and high prices are often mistaken for indicators of a work's aesthetic value.[10]

The ability of large auction houses to shape taste, make reputations and set market trends is undeniable, but this is only part of the picture. Increasingly, the auction format is being appropriated and transformed by those who work outside the upper echelons of the international art market. While some innovative auction activities are undertaken by artists, individuals and collectives in emulation of top-tier businesses, others are designed as a subversion of them. Experimentation with this historic sales format attests further to the contemporary importance of art auctions and broadens the remit of their spectacle. Arguably, the more dominant a set of norms, the stronger is the incentive to devise and implement counter-cultural strategies. As the following chapters will demonstrate, the auction has become a surprisingly mutable format in the 21st century and is capable of both reinforcing and challenging preconceptions about art markets and the values they create or perpetuate.

Whether large or small, international or regional, auction houses are always keen to launch new initiatives. The 21st century has witnessed the development of novel, online sales formats as well as innovative collaborations between auction businesses, artists, collectors and museums. Increasingly, some of these strategies are bringing about structural changes in the art market itself. Auctions have historically been associated with the secondary market – a sphere in which transactions take place after an artwork's first acquisition by, for example, a collector, gallerist or museum (a primary market sale).[11] While I will examine some of the culturally specific issues that impact on the firmness of the distinction between these market segments, it is widely recognised that auction houses around the world have encroached on the primary market by facilitating sales direct from artists to publics. In some senses, private sales on the part of auction houses are nothing new. They can help to prop up an auction house's balance sheet when the secondary market is thin, and the 1990s saw both Sotheby's and Christie's move into this arena.[12] Increasingly, however, auction houses are collaborating with, and selling works by, living artists, thereby usurping the traditional role of gallerists as those artists' representatives. While this can lead to productive collaboration by auction houses with both artists and their gallerists, it has also generated tensions that I will examine in different art-world contexts.

Market expansion is matched by transformations in the cultural positioning of auction houses. No longer simply places for transacting in art, many of these businesses are styling themselves as multi-purpose cultural centres with spaces for exhibitions, education and public engagement. Such activities are often matched by the commissioning of new architecture and the resulting transformation of built environments. Taken together, these strategic innovations mark a significant extension of auction businesses and a spectacular reshaping of familiar cultural economies.

### Auctions and Art Worlds

Throughout the following discussion I will explore the role that auctions – and ideas about them – play in so-called 'art worlds'. In his elaboration of this term, sociologist Howard S. Becker sought to identify and map socially cooperative activities that are necessary to support conceptions of both art and artists. He argued that works of art are not just singular artefacts produced by gifted individuals. Rather, they are the 'joint products' of people who cooperate through certain conventions to bring such works into existence.[13] From here, he continues, we 'look for other people who are also necessary to that production, gradually building up as complete a picture as we can of the entire cooperating network that radiates out from the work in question'.[14] The result is an 'art world' comprised of institutions and individuals who, acting together, generate knowledge frameworks and social customs that make the very idea of art possible. Auctions, and the people who participate in them, are key players in these cooperative networks.

Over the course of five chapters, I examine auctions at the nexus of spectacle and value in a variety of art worlds. Chapter 1 surveys the evolution of auction-room drama from its origins to the rise of digital environments. While online and hybrid auctions have offered international businesses a new way of marketing and selling art, the internet is also a tool that artists and communities use to adapt the auction format for their own purposes. This suggests a certain democratisation of auctions and a broadening of access to formerly exclusive spaces for the exchange of art. In Chapter 2 I turn to the expansion of auction models across borders and discuss tensions that arise when this sales format is transposed to different cultural and regional contexts. In such cases, auction activity can produce results that may seem minor when viewed from an international perspective, but are spectacular in local contexts. Chapter 3 delves further into the creation of value by exploring how auctions leverage celebrity and data in their increasingly sophisticated marketing materials. By exploiting a highly networked information economy, auction houses ignite the passion for collecting among their clients while also extending their reach both culturally and financially. This leads to a discussion in Chapter 4 of the role played by auction houses in developing new exhibition cultures and creating changes in urban environments. I conclude by examining various controversies to which auctions give rise and debate how these resonate throughout art worlds.

This book does not aim to offer a global survey of art auctions. Instead, I have selected cases that exemplify significant trends in contemporary market environments. My hope is to highlight the diversity of auctions while drawing out points of contrast and entanglement. This also entails consideration of the dematerialised spectacle to which art auctions give rise, including the production of knowledge and news. Throughout the discussion, I emphasise that auctions are far more than economic mechanisms for transacting in precious artefacts. They are also important platforms for human interaction. Whether propelling the ebbs and flows of artists' careers, showcasing the private passions of collectors or simply generating events for people to watch in person or online, auctions constitute a spectacular sphere of information about art and its values in the 21st century.

# 1

# Auction as Spectacle

Auctions come in many formats and, in their earliest incarnations, were mechanisms for the transfer of goods, disposal of the spoils of war and, tragically, exchange of people as chattels. By the 17th century, auctions had become a convenient forum for transacting in estate sales and objects in markets with strong collector bases such as books. As the popularity of auctions grew, specialist operations came into being to promote trade and regularise the rules of sale. In 1674 the then governor of Stockholm, Baron Claes Rålamb, opened the first European auction house – Auktionsverk – a business that remains in operation today.[1] Just over thirty years later, the Dorotheum was founded by Emperor Joseph I in Vienna. From its origins as a pawn brokerage and organiser of estate sales, the operation blossomed into one of the largest auction houses in the world.[2] In the United Kingdom, public art auctions were held from the 1680s onwards, but it was the 18th century that witnessed the emergence of businesses that would become lasting players: Sotheby's (1744), Christie's (1766), Bonhams (1793) and Phillips (1796).[3] By the time the Hôtel Drouot was created in Paris in 1852, the auction had become a staple element of a recognisably modern art trade.

Auctions are closely intertwined with histories of shipping, migration and colonisation. As the major trading centre of Northern Italy, Venice was the site of art auctions as early as the 15th century, while in Amsterdam (another key trading centre) auctions specialising in art took place from 1608 onwards.[4] Port life also influenced the emergence of art auctions in the United States. In 1805 the print seller Tristram Bampfylde Freeman journeyed from London to Philadelphia and began holding textile auctions in a popular meeting place, Merchant's Coffee House. Capitalising on the city's shipping trade, the family-owned Freeman's auction house gradually expanded its business through sales of imported goods as well as real estate and, eventually, art.[5]

The development of art markets in Australia and China demonstrates a further transfer of the auction concept from Britain to new cultural contexts. Focusing on Australia, Shireen Huda explores the auction as part of a colonial project that began with imported objects and social hierarchies from Europe: while auctions of paintings were associated with the tastes and leisure pursuits of the 'upper classes', general auctions were thought better suited for 'lower classes'.[6] Although local auction houses came into being in Australia from the 1850s onwards, these businesses traded primarily in European art and works produced by the descendants of European settlers. It was not until the 1980s that a market for Indigenous art emerged, with Sotheby's first specialised 'Aboriginal art auction' taking place in Melbourne on 30 June 1997.[7]

The dominant style of art auction to emerge from these different ventures was one in which bids are made verbally and proceed in an ascending sequence – the so-called 'English' auction.[8] As a public event, this kind of sale was designed to encourage open (though not necessarily transparent) competition among bidders for the purpose of driving up prices. Yet throughout their various histories, auctions have rarely been held simply for the benefit of sellers, potential buyers or, indeed, auction houses themselves. Appealing to the interest of curious onlookers, these sales generate virtual tourism in which the personal histories of individuals and families are opened to a public gaze. Cynthia Wall states in her study of British 18th-century auctions that individuals from a range of social classes could enjoy opportunities to view and, in some cases, acquire 'the fragments of another's life' for the purpose of shaping their own.[9] While buying at auction may only have been open to those with means, the visual spectacle of auctions – including the pre-sale display of goods – had much wider appeal. In the 18th century, Wall notes, 'Anything, anywhere, anytime, seemed to be up for sale'.[10]

## Showbiz

Creating bespoke environments for the exhibition of goods both before and during an auction contributes strongly to the spectacle of this sales format. Writing about auctions staged by Thomas Kirby for the American Art Association in New York during the latter decades of the 19th century, John Ott describes how auctioneers designed increasingly theatrical environments to celebrate Gilded Age wealth and collections.[11] From sumptuous sales rooms to liveried porters and the cultivation of close media relationships, Kirby created a transactional space that showcased the refined sensibilities and collecting habits of his clients. Kirby's tactics were also designed to interest broader audiences in this branch of exclusive art collecting, but the latter's role was to witness rather than to participate in the proceedings.

Techniques for harnessing the power of visual spectacle to generate interest in art commerce received a major boost in the 20th century with developments in mass media. One of the most famous auctions to harness the power of the press was Sotheby's stunning black-tie evening sale held at its Bond Street sales rooms on 15 October 1958. Featuring Impressionist and modern art drawn from the collection of the late financier Jakob Goldschmidt, the glamorous auction was stage-managed and marketed by Sotheby's then chairman, Peter Wilson. The flamboyant Wilson had served as an intelligence officer during the Second World War and was also a friend of the British spy novelist Ian Fleming. Art writer Philip Hook credits Wilson with transforming the auction house 'into something that directly rivalled and even usurped the function of the art dealer' by establishing a glamorous forum in which to secure the highest prices for art.[12] In 1962 British *Vogue* styled Wilson as 'something of a masterpiece' himself and – in keeping with the exercise of verbal wit long associated with the practice of the auctioneer – a salesman capable of encouraging 'unheard of bids of art'.[13]

Aside from its art-market success, the Goldschmidt sale was a media triumph. Wilson had mounted an extensive publicity campaign, successfully building heat for the event.[14] On the evening of the sale, a well-heeled audience rubbed shoulders with celebrities including actors (Anthony Quinn and Kirk Douglas), writers (William Somerset Maugham), socialites (Lady Churchill) and the prima ballerina Dame Margot Fonteyn. Hollywood actor Edward G. Robinson – onscreen gangster and offscreen art collector – participated via telephone from the US.[15] Photographers, reporters and a television crew documented the applause as new sales records were set. Legend has it that police had to hold back a crowd of curious onlookers.

This spectacular auction appealed to buyers and sellers, but it was also designed to publicise the idea of the auction and its capacity to play a leading role in the market. The illustrated London magazine *The Sphere* described the event as the 'Sale of the Century', reporting that seven works achieved an aggregate sales price of £781,000 (just over £15 million today) in a mere 21 minutes.[16] According to the *Illustrated London News*, only 400 people could be accommodated in the main gallery, while over a thousand others watched the proceedings on 'thirteen television sets relaying on closed circuit the exciting scene in the main room'.[17] The art auction had entered the era of mass media spectacle.

## Going Digital

If the setting of the auction house and the theatrical choreography of its action are central to both its social function and economic model, what happens when a pandemic forces art audiences into their homes and requires businesses and cultural institutions to shutter their doors? Historically, art markets have survived – and in many cases thrived – on adversity. Disruptions caused by war, the forced displacement of individuals, and the waxing and waning of private fortunes are just some of the factors that bring artworks onto the auction market. COVID-19 was unusual, however, in that it was global and took individuals, communities and businesses by surprise in the extent of its virulence and capacity to generate uncertainty.

International auction houses needed to innovate swiftly, and the digital realm seemed to provide an obvious solution. Online offerings were already a familiar aspect of art sales. Artists and gallerists had become accustomed to showcasing works on Instagram; Sotheby's had experimented with online auctions during the 1990s in partnership with Amazon and eBay; Saatchi Online was founded by advertising mogul Charles Saatchi in 2006; Artsy, created in 2009 by US computer scientist Carter Cleveland, began brokering art online in 2012.[18] In the case of international art auctions, however, even the most sophisticated technologies were not a simple panacea. Online trading might have seemed an obvious solution to a physically depopulated art world, but it lacked the glamour, community and spectacle of the black-tie evening sale.

By spring 2020, auction houses were gambling on strategies that were likely to affect their long-term prospects as trusted players in the art market. While they were accustomed to estimating the price of art, they now needed to put a value on different aspects of their own businesses. That involved thinking innovatively about how to maintain effective connections with existing clients while attracting new audiences. Developing a suitable online platform for the exchange of multi-million-pound artworks meant that auction houses had to identify those elements of their sales models that best communicated to publics. Would people risk bidding on a work that they had seen only in virtual reality? Would sellers want some of their most precious possessions 'reduced' to jpegs in a screen-based environment? How could art-world sociability be maintained in such circumstances?

According to information gathered by the art data research firm Pi-eX: 'From mid-March to the end of May 2020, Christie's, Sotheby's, and Phillips cancelled more than 90 scheduled live auctions and created or rescheduled more than 100 online only auctions'.[19] Yet an exclusively online format that invited bids solely at the click of a button lacked the thrill of the traditional auction experience. Where was the sales narrative that maximised the drama of competitive bidding? It soon became clear that the prices achieved in online auctions did not match the financial returns of live events.[20] It was imperative to create a new kind of spectacle.

In the summer of 2020, Sotheby's launched a hybrid event that it billed as 'the first sale of its kind'.[21] Titled 'From Rembrandt to Richter', the event included a live auctioneer and auction-house specialists, but solicited online and telephone bidding from participants. If the format was good enough for works by one of the most historically sought-after European painters (Rembrandt van Rijn) and a living artist who achieves some of the highest grossing sales prices for his art (Gerhard Richter), surely potential buyers would be reassured by the arrangement? An immersive digital catalogue comprising 71 lots offered the opportunity to take a virtual tour of Sotheby's showroom. High-quality reproductions of paintings, timelines and videos enhanced the online experience, with an augmented-reality app enabling viewers to see how a work might look in their homes.

The question remained as to how the spectacle of the traditional sales format could be replicated in this online setting? A new visual strategy was required to galvanise and hold the interest of both sellers and bidders. The solution was the introduction of an energetic performance capable of transforming an individual's solitary, on-screen experience into something unexpectedly social and visually arresting. Instead of maintaining the traditional set-up of the auction room with the auctioneer in front of an audience, the online spectacle exploited a roving camera angle and multi-screen stage. Cameras directed attention to auction-house specialists wearing watches and jewellery scheduled to feature in upcoming sales. The traditional theatrical environment was flipped so that viewers could see the room (in this case a set of screens in different locations) from the perspective of the auctioneer. The new, dematerialised art auction was an opportunity to pull back the curtain and show the backstage workings of the sale from unconventional angles that included sight of the auctioneer's teleprompter.

Auctioneers themselves were endowed with enhanced celebrity status as they took centre stage in this dynamic event and its online press materials. Dirk Boll of Christie's has described the auctioneer as an 'heroic' character who exploits the 'visceral fascination' that competitive sales exert on the public imagination.[22] Livestreamed events that attracted audiences and viewers from around the world expanded the auctioneer's remit. Directing audience attention across multiple monitors, the auctioneer now had to generate tension, banter with colleagues, improvise and control the flow of bidding in ways that Sotheby's auctioneer Oliver Barker described as analogous to a 'cinematic production'.[23] By July 2020, *The New York Times* wondered whether the art auction had entered the era of the 'game show' with auctioneers the new 'hosts'.[24]

The summer of 2020 saw Christie's initiate its own version of this multi-site adventure when it announced a modern and contemporary sale in the form of a 'global live auction' or 'relay' between Hong Kong, Paris, London and New York. Rather than placing the event in the hands of one auctioneer, this format saw the gavel-cum-baton passed between sales personnel in each location. The continuity of the design across time zones was designed to encourage longer engagement on the part of spectators, sellers or bidders who could 'go home for dinner and watch it [the auction] unfold online, bidding from their own sitting room'.[25] Art dealer Jeffrey Deitch billed the sale as one of the 'greatest shows on earth', while Alex Rotter (Chairman of Post-War and Contemporary Art, Christie's New York) announced that the auction house was breaking 'the calendar, the rules and the very concept of the auction'.[26]

Whereas audiences had typically been brought together in the sales room, they were now linked virtually across different continents. This electronic replication of an international art-world community mapped neatly onto major financial centres around the world. Evidencing Boltanski and Esquerre's argument that major auction houses have the capacity to create a unified market 'from above',[27] livestreamed proceedings from London, New York, Paris and Hong Kong reinforced a network of elite consumption that connected financial hubs. The pandemic gave auction houses an opportunity to position themselves visually as linchpins in a global market.

### Who Wants to be a Millionaire?

Recordings of online art auctions show audiences chatting about the proceedings, debating prices and sometimes commenting on auction-house personnel. Livestreamed sales are also bookended with interviews and commemorated by online catalogues and other digital material. If printed auction catalogues with telling annotations by bidders constitute an important archive of art commerce, digital objects now document the unfolding history of the market. Do these online sales formats suggest new avenues for participation in the art world when compared to the traditionally closed – and arguably more intimidating – space of the physical sales room?

Creating new purchasing opportunities seems like common sense for any business, but there are countervailing issues in the case of the art auction. Central to this is the social dynamic of the auction environment itself. While auctions may span a range of artefacts and prices, the international art market is, of necessity, interested in attracting the highest bids for works it deems not just the best available, but the best in history. That means maintaining the interest of high-net-worth buyers and sellers and creating a social environment that appeals to them.

Despite the pressures of an increasingly strict lockdown, Sotheby's 'Rembrandt to Richter' sale included an on-site dinner at the London premises for a small number of socially distanced clients who enjoyed 'a curated selection of Sotheby's wines' as they watched the event unfold.[28] The tempering of a mass, online spectacle with a reserved (physical) space for elite consumption demonstrated a desire to maintain the aura of the traditional format even while embracing the new. Mass spectatorship was welcome, provided it was kept within bounds.

Although international auction houses championed online platforms during the pandemic, the acts of observing and participating remained as clearly partitioned as they were in the 19th century. Indeed, the presence of larger, anonymous audiences drawn from around the world intensified this discrepancy: individuals from contrasting socio-economic backgrounds could now come together to watch the circulation of expensive art in an international sales arena without impinging on the privacy of bidders who remained in their own homes. By creating a global audience for auctions and encouraging spectatorship through online chat, auction houses at the top of the market used the digital realm to fulfil one of the historically important features of their business model: the demarcation of a space in which to showcase the habits and tastes of the wealthy.

Since the pandemic lockdowns, livestreamed international art auctions have continued in online formats or as hybrid events that include both remote and in-person audiences. Statistics suggest that while online auctions dominated the 2020 market, the balance between online and in-person sales stabilised to a more even split in post-pandemic conditions.[29] As a newly established feature of art-world spectacle, these sales often attract viewers in excess of 100,000, with some events achieving far higher figures. Christie's estimated that its 2022 sale of art, antiques and furniture from the collection of fashion icon Hubert de Givenchy attracted 1.3 million viewers from around the world.[30] This marks a significant extension of the art market's reach and its role in popular culture. Whereas police had to control bystanders at Sotheby's 1958 Goldschmidt sale, auction houses can now encourage a potentially limitless global audience to witness the spectacle of their trade.

## Widening Opportunity

Discussions about art auctions often focus on the activities of the largest international players. Yet many other institutions and collectives have taken advantage of online formats to widen the range of commercial opportunities available to artists, sellers and collectors. The pandemic accelerated these developments across the market spectrum. In a report on French auction businesses published in 2022, the online sale of art was described not as a mere 'trend', but as a 'fully-fledged digital revolution'. It was estimated that online sales of art rose by 83 per cent between 2020 and 2021 in France, with those at the historic Hôtel Drouot – strategically rebranded as Drouot Digital – having grown by 211 per cent between 2019 and 2021.[31]

The dramatic rise in online and hybrid auctions is, however, more than a story about sales figures or technology. It reveals wider ambitions across the sector to remodel the format of the art auction and to use it for the purpose of introducing new artists, artworks and audiences to the market. If international auction businesses have historically required sustained interest from an elite cadre of buyers and sellers, aggregator platforms that showcase art at a wide range of price points or that present multiple events simultaneously can generate interest by virtue of scale. Bidspirit (created in Israel in 2012) is a portal that unites selected auction sales of art and other collectibles in a range of countries and facilitates online bidding. In similar fashion, France's Interenchères (created in the early 2000s) unites individual lots on a single platform, livestreams sales events and advertises 'classical' (in-person) sales. For any armchair bidder familiar with eBay, these online offerings are an easy means of browsing and buying art at a range of different price points. Clare McAndrew notes that aggregator sites are an important marketing forum for smaller businesses and that platforms such as Invaluable and Liveauctioneers can 'rival some of the top-tier auction houses in the sector'.[32]

While it is difficult to establish parameters that enable like-for-like comparisons between these businesses and their large competitors, the point remains that the format of the online auction facilitates a range of marketing opportunities designed to broaden access to art and art buying. Evidencing this spirit of inclusivity, South Korea's Seoul Auction, founded in 1998, announced its ambition to 'embrace all generations' by offering online and offline auctions that reflect a range of tastes and budgets. Its use of technology to discharge interlinked missions of popularising and revitalising art and culture exemplifies the wider aims of this strategy.[33]

The successful staging of online auctions requires ease of use and administration. Many such events have a fixed period for bidding and allocate the lot to the highest bidder at a particular cut-off time. These are modern versions of so-called 'candle auctions', popular in the 17th and 18th centuries, in which bidding ended when a candle expired. This added a lottery element to the proceedings, as bidders had to keep an eye not only on their competitors, but also on the likely timing of their bids. Whether the life of the event is limited by a candle or an algorithm, it is possible to be outbid by a rival who slips in an offer just before the bidding period expires (an act known as 'sniping'). In an attempt to counter this problem, some online auctions (such as those run by Artsy) add an additional time period if bidding takes place in the closing minutes.

An alternative approach is the 'Dutch auction', a sale that proceeds in reverse fashion with an opening price that decreases as time passes. In this case, bidders must balance the lure of a lower price with the risk of losing to someone who jumps in to accept the slowly descending offer. This format has also been tried in digital form. In some of its events, Singulart (founded in France in 2017) fuses Dutch and candle auctions in online sales during which the price of an artwork metaphorically 'melts' as time passes.[34] As Charles W. Smith notes, however, when the first bid is quite possibly the last, there is reason to doubt whether this kind of sale is, in fact, a competitive auction.[35]

## Open Doors

Developments in art auctions have not simply been propelled by new technologies, the evolution of business models or the desire to attract broader audiences. They have also been motivated by a drive to extend the practice of auctioneering. In some cases, this means that the auction format is seized by new hands. In 2017 former Christie's auctioneer, Tom Best, created the UK-based Auction Collective to 'open up the auction model' by helping artists, institutions and charities run their own professional events.[36] The Auction Collective signals a growing interest among individuals and groups to preserve the spectacle of the auction while adapting it to suit their own needs.

In such cases, artists and artworks from a range of backgrounds can attract new publics. The digital platform Ans Azura (founded by Suzana Vasilescu and Andreea Stanculeanu in 2021) holds both online and livestreamed auctions to publicise and sell art from Central Eastern Europe and the Middle East. Here, as elsewhere, there is a focus on educating and attracting new audiences to 'engage with art and learn about collecting'.[37] Evidencing a similar ambition, the Swedish photographer Gustav Almestål and art director Hedvig Myhrman developed an auction format on Instagram during the pandemic: S.Y.L.A. (Support Your Local Artist). The platform was designed to solicit bids via Instagram and, one hour before the auction slot for a specific work ended, participants were connected in a thread, with the highest bidder winning the work. Although the formats of Ans Azura and S.Y.L.A. may be simple, the idea behind them is important: the competitive spectacle of the auction is understood as an important means of advertising art in addition to selling it. The social power of the auction makes it an effective vehicle for generating collective knowledge about art and artists.

Although the appetite for online and hybrid auctions across all segments of the market suggests that this kind of sale is an enticement to buyers, sellers and publics, the diversity of formats and approaches does not suggest a unified trajectory. The key challenge for international auction houses has been to balance the allure of tradition with the vitality of the new. For individual artists and collectives, by contrast, the internet offers an independent conduit to markets. While auction spectacle continues to be fuelled by new uses of technology, this sales format also evolves through border crossing, regional development and the contestation of familiar market divisions. I now turn to a range of partnerships and rivalries that are arising in the rapidly expanding auction environment of the 21st century.

# 2

# Expanding Markets

Art-market data reveals that the US, China and the UK were the three leaders in the global art-auction market in 2022, with the majority of highest-priced works having been sold in New York.[1] Although this information reveals activity at the top end of the international art market, it does not give a full sense of the reach of art auctions or of the role they play in wider social contexts. I now want to consider the kinds of spectacle that auctions create when they are transposed to new settings. Do they support local ideas about the values attaching to art or do they sow disruption? What happens when auction houses extend their reach by seeking sources of supply in untapped segments of the art market? Answering these questions entails thinking about auctions as rules-based events that mediate ideas about art across cultures.

## Creating Art Genres

Auction houses – particularly those capable of operating at scale – open up markets and, in some cases, bring new kinds of art to public attention through sophisticated branding, networking and communication techniques. Leili Sreberny-Mohammadi has examined the important role played by Christie's in developing art markets in Dubai since the business established itself there in 2006.[2] In parallel with the rise of art fairs and commercial galleries in the Emirates, Christie's capitalised on a growing base of local collectors while also promoting Middle Eastern art and Iranian art in wider art economies. According to Sreberny-Mohammadi, the auction house viewed itself as doing more than simply making a market for particular kinds of art. Rather it sought to act as a productive contributor to the creation of a new regional art world.[3]

It is undoubtedly the case that major auction houses have the capacity and resources to bring artists to public attention and stage events that appeal to a wide range of collector classes. To what extent, however, do these activities contribute to the creation of lasting and stable regional art cultures? Although international auction houses may expand into new markets, they are businesses that are, of necessity, geared towards profit rather than the long-term cultivation of local art infrastructures. In her study of the global art trade, Larissa Buchholz argues that auction houses 'are notorious for their focus on short-term profits, and they often cherry-pick single artworks that promise high sales revenues rather than making a sustained commitment to representing an artist's entire body of work, as galleries tend to do'.[4] Auction houses identify demand for art, yet opinion divides on the role they play in the expansion of art worlds.

In an interview of 2018, art critic and co-director of Assar Art Gallery in Iran, Maryam Majd, spoke of the difficulties she encountered in her attempts to promote emerging artists through international auction-house platforms. Failing to capitalise on Christie's marketing of Iranian art following the house's opening in Dubai, Majd commented that 'we were completely on the wrong track – on the other side of the coin; so, we immediately switched tracks by only including masterpieces – not young artists – when we participated'.[5] Majd's comments suggest that a close connection between auction houses, commercial galleries and contemporary artists can put at risk the longer-term support needed to assist artists by privileging a narrow cadre of individuals whose works are deemed 'saleable' in an auction setting.

Speaking from a different perspective, Iranian sculptor Parviz Tanavoli credits Christie's with shining an international spotlight on Iranian art, a step that he feels benefitted both emerging *and* established artists by encouraging local and international buyers and, more importantly, raising wider awareness of Iranian art.[6] The views of Majd and Tanavoli demonstrate the contrasting expectations and needs of different art-world participants, but also signal the powerful role that large auction houses play when they move into regional art economies.

Dirk Boll of Christie's confirms the balancing act that is required when expanding into new regions.[7] There is, as he puts it, a 'soft spot' where a type of art or art movement is known well enough by audiences to generate sustained demand. When that soft spot is found, the benefits can extend to the primary market by, for example, 'validating' the works in which gallerists trade and providing the latter with public prices that can serve as benchmarks for their own sales activities. Answering the question I posed at the beginning of this chapter about the potential of auction houses to mediate ideas about art across cultural boundaries, Boll described Christie's Dubai venture as the creation of a regional 'hub' that attracted local collectors as well as those from neighbouring countries. Not only was the auction model itself recognised as a sales arena that followed a set of international standards, but wider events and exhibition activities organised by the auction house expanded the range of regional cultural offerings. In this case, an auction business functioned as significantly more than a transactional platform.

### Inside Out

Where does the promotion of art categories by international auction houses leave regional businesses? Continuing the theme of Iranian art, Tehran Auction was established in 2012 by Alireza Sami Azar (former head of Tehran's Museum of Contemporary Art). If Christie's established an international category of modern and contemporary Iranian art as an internationally marketable commodity from a position outside the country, Tehran Auction's aim is to work from inside out. In marketing material, it describes its ambition 'to support the *domestic* art market as a key basis for the international market' (emphasis added).[8]

The opening event staged in 2012 was reported as the first contemporary art auction in Iran and, more importantly, as a 'symbol of the burgeoning self-confidence of the country's art scene'.[9] Bearing out this view, 73 lots were sold for an aggregate amount of approximately US$1.7 million. At the auction held in July 2023, 100 out of 110 works were sold, netting total sales proceeds of just over US$4.2 million.[10] These figures may not rival those of major auctions in established art-market hubs, but they generate considerable local spectacle by virtue of their staging and press coverage.[11] In 2014 Michelle Moghtader noted that only about 10 per cent of the 1000 attendees at that year's Tehran Auction placed a bid, but that the event was, nevertheless, 'very much a place to see and be seen'.[12] Although Iran has been subject to significant political upheaval and has had to negotiate the impact of international economic sanctions for many decades, it is an important testing ground for opportunities and power shifts created by the emergence of an art auction scene that continues to develop within and outside the country's borders.[13]

## Validation or Volatility?

Auction houses may position themselves as conduits to wider markets, but this can also generate art-world volatility. Businesses have been known to back out of markets as swiftly as they sought to enter them. In 1994 Christie's was the first international auction house to establish a presence in India. Filip Vermeylen used this example to suggest that India, like other countries in the Global South, had adopted a Western model of market organisation comprising auction houses, commercial gallerists, fairs and foreign intermediaries to generate an art business.[14] In 2017 (two years after Vermeylen's analysis was published), Christie's ceased holding live auctions in India. What might this suggest about the relationship between local and global art landscapes and the role of auction houses as a junction point between them?

Christie's closed its business in India, but continues to hold auctions of Indian art in its other offices, highlighting that maintaining a market for art production associated with a particular country does not necessarily require a physical presence there. Nor did Christie's decision to leave this market reflect an absence of local interest in either art or art commerce. Sotheby's continues to have a presence in India, and there remain other important Mumbai-based auction houses including AstaGuru, Pundole's and Saffronart. Saffronart was established in 2000, while AstaGuru and Pundole's followed in 2008 and 2011 respectively. In her analysis of this cultural environment, Olga Kanzaki Sooudi points to the uneven emergence of local 'validating institutions' in India and the pressures felt from an increasingly global market:

> Despite Indian art worlds' long history, artists, gallerists, curators and others felt that their world was new because much of the current art world had come into being following market growth in and after the 1990s. This new art world is a globalised one centred around the private sector, and insiders felt older institutions such as the art school or museum had failed to meet its needs.[15]

Auction houses contribute to the kaleidoscope of validating institutions that Sooudi identifies as important to the creation of an Indian art world, yet they often promote styles of art that will sell internationally. While auctions may implement recognisable rules for art transactions and draw local art production into a global dialogue, this can contribute to a 'geography of prestige', as Sooudi puts it, that relies on validation from outside the local context.[16]

In his study of art worlds in Nigeria, Jonathan Adeyemi points out a similar set of issues. He describes Nigeria's contemporary art market as having been 'auction driven' and connects this to the adoption of a 'Western' auction model that promotes modern and contemporary art from West Africa.[17] Arthouse Contemporary (launched in 2008) was the country's first auction house and, according to its founder Kavita

Chellaram, was conceived as a response to the then 'unstructured state' of the art market in Nigeria. As in India, the auction model is used as a mechanism to create validation for the benefit of art and artists in the country. According to Adeyemi, the auction house contributes to a market success story that has encouraged collector confidence, internationalisation and opportunities in the primary market. Yet he also reports a discussion with one Nigerian artist who admits to creating work primarily for the two auctions held annually by Arthouse Contemporary.[18] This raises the question whether an auction-driven market imbues the relevant businesses with unwarranted levels of power to shape not just local art worlds, but also the creative practices of those who inhabit them.

Auction houses seeking to expand regional art worlds often cultivate relationships with local communities and try to open new opportunities for audience engagement. The South African auction house Strauss Art, for example, complements its primary businesses in Johannesburg and Cape Town with teacher training and drawing workshops as well as an 'Art Club'. Extending roots into the market for emerging artists, Freeman's auction house in Philadelphia (mentioned in Chapter 1) collaborated in 2022 with the Pennsylvania Academy of the Fine Arts to host an exhibition of works by Master of Fine Arts graduates.[19] Operating on a larger scale, in 2023 Sotheby's was an official supporting partner of the inaugural Islamic Arts Biennale held at the King Abdulaziz International Airport in Jeddah, Saudi Arabia. In its press release, the auction house emphasised its contribution to the creation of 'global cultural dialogue and awareness', including a commitment to supporting 'educational outreach and diversifying cultural initiatives' in the Middle East.[20] Strategies such as these suggest that auction houses benefit from extending beyond commercial contexts. Whether creating new networks or helping to develop an infrastructure to support their core activities, auction houses are exerting increasing levels of cultural authority by shaping the frameworks of knowledge and interpretation in which art is experienced, understood and valued.

**Eroding Boundaries**

While regional auction houses often serve local communities, many of them seek to attain greater market visibility through strategic partnerships. In 2000 Freeman's entered into a marketing alliance with the oldest Scottish auction house, Lyon & Turnbull, and in 2023 merged with the Chicago-based Hindman Auctions to form Freeman's | Hindman.[21] In 2022 Bonhams acquired the Massachusetts-based Skinner auction house as well as Bruun Rasmussen in Copenhagen and the leading Nordic auction house, Bukowskis. In a similar vein, France's Artcurial, founded in 2002, has expanded from a Paris-based operation to become one of the world's largest auction businesses. It is worth noting that, aside from Paris, its offices are in cities outside traditional centres of the international art market. Focusing on Brussels, Milan, Monaco, Marrakech and Munich shifts attention from sales environments dominated by Christie's, Sotheby's and Phillips. Through its acquisition of Beurret Bailly Widmer in Basel in 2023, Artcurial also strategically positions itself in relation to one of the world's major art fairs, Art Basel, and held its 'Modern and Contemporary Art' auction sale during the fair in 2023.

Auction houses and art fairs have not, however, always enjoyed an easy relationship. Art fairs developed, in part, to offer gallerists a bulwark against the power and international reach of large auction houses. Alain Quemin points out in his recent study of contemporary galleries that tensions came to the fore in the mid-1990s when the major art fairs, Art Basel, Art Cologne, Chicago Art Fair, FIAC (Foire internationale d'art contemporain) and ARCOmadrid united to form the International Contemporary Art Fair Association to regulate access to their events and to keep auction houses at bay.[22] When Christie's acquired the London gallery Haunch of Venison in 2007, the gallery (now closed) was promptly excluded from Frieze and Art Basel's group of fairs.[23] Battles for turf still exist, but there is much evidence to suggest that familiar boundaries are eroding.

Auction houses typically hold lectures, give tours and seek to attract clients during the run of a fair. Recently, however, closer interaction has evolved between market players. Auction house Bolsa de Arte, based in Rio de Janeiro and São Paulo, describes its twinned aims as 'the dissemination of works by national artists inside and outside the country, and participation in art fairs'.[24] On a more local level, Bonhams partners with the Fresh Art Fair in Cheltenham and Ascot in the UK on events that generate opportunities for potential sellers and brand enhancement for the auction house.[25] Christie's is an official partner of 1-54, an important African art fair that takes its name from the 54 countries of the African continent. Publicity for the 2023 iteration of the event in London described the partnership as signalling 'the fair's strong and dynamic relationship with the global auction house'.[26] Coupled with Christie's pop-up exhibition titled *1-54 Presents* at its London premises, there is evidence to suggest that a more synergistic art world is evolving.

In an important step in India, an art fair – Art Mumbai – was inaugurated in 2023. Attracting gallerists from India and abroad, the fair is the brainchild of Dinesh Vazirani, a co-founder of the Indian auction house Saffronart. In press reports, Vazirani has stated that the two businesses will remain separate.[27] It is noteworthy, however, that this foray into the art-fair circuit comes from the world of auctions rather than from private sales. It is symptomatic of much bigger shifts that are taking place between once distinct market sectors.

### New Commercial Landscapes

There have been many headlines in the art press over the last five years about auction houses 'gatecrashing' the primary market by working directly with artists on sales of their output.[28] There are, however, cultural specificities to consider in connection with this development. China, for example, has long been known for its use of auctions as arenas for the display and sale of art direct from artists' studios. Svetlana Kharchenkova and Olav Velthuis have examined the use of auctions in China as 'marketing devices' that make artworks visible in ways that commercial art galleries in the country do not.[29] The analysis reveals widespread confidence in the role of auction houses in China, the latter's historically strong ties to the state helping to establish them as trusted 'judgment devices' for collectors.[30] Kharchenkova and Velthuis's study concerned the first decade of the 21st century, and the authors anticipated that the local dominance of auction houses would wane as China became increasingly integrated into global art-market practices and norms. Yet, there is evidence to suggest that Chinese auction houses are continuing to expand their reach both internally and abroad.

Philip Dodd (former Director of London's Institute of Contemporary Arts and Chairman of Made in China UK Ltd) points out the immense popularity of auctions (of all kinds) in China, with art functioning, at times, as a major investment vehicle for individuals based in and outside the country's major cities.[31] In Dodd's view, auction houses began playing a major role in the country during the 1990s because they filled a gap in the prevailing 'commercial ecology', a period that saw very few galleries and no museums of contemporary art. Nearly thirty years later, the country's art landscape has changed dramatically and has witnessed the building of a huge number of public museums, the emergence of private museums, the blossoming of Chinese and foreign galleries and the establishment of art fairs and biennials.[32] These developments have by no means weakened the auction market. On the contrary, while niche auction houses continue to flourish, some of the largest businesses, including China Guardian and Poly Auction, promote both traditional and contemporary Chinese art to local collectors while also targeting overseas expansion and the sourcing of works from Western consignors.[33]

Dodd also points out that a new player has emerged in this fast-paced environment and that it has the potential to transform auction markets: the Chinese-owned company, TikTok. TikTok (Douyin in China) has become a popular marketing platform for auction houses, with both Sotheby's and Christie's gaining considerable traction by uploading footage from high-profile sales.[34] But Dodd points out that with TikTok itself operating as a major e-commerce platform in China, its capacity to host auctions in its own right has the potential to create a major shift in the market.[35] With over 1 billion active monthly users globally as of 2023 – and around 750 million monthly active users of Douyin in China – this social media platform might not simply enhance opportunities for art commerce and taste-making, but also open new spheres of value that change the balance of power in the global art landscape.

### Redefining the Primary Market

In 2019 Seoul Auction launched an online platform titled Zero Base to promote work by emerging artists. Strikingly, this was a sales event that opened bidding with a starting price of zero as a reflection of the artists' newness to the market.[36] This initiative was, however, part of a trend that troubled commercial gallerists. In 2022 the Galleries Association of Korea issued a statement to both Seoul Auction and the country's other major auction house, K Auction, in which it was alleged that both businesses were threatening the prospects of commercial galleries by collaborating with emerging talent.[37] In a spirit of retaliation, the Galleries Association staged its own auction at the Westin Josun Seoul hotel and allegedly succeeded in selling 95 per cent of the 117 lots for sale.[38]

While such a tussle for market share is a familiar component of institutionally complex financial environments, e-commerce once again comes to the fore as a means of propelling new developments. To take one example, Phillips launched Dropshop in 2023 – an operation that claims to redefine 'the dynamics between the primary and secondary art markets' by offering regularly scheduled 'drops' of works on its digital platform. Instead of an auction, this is a 'buy now' model that is intended to 'modernize the collecting experience'.[39] Importantly, the venture includes a benefit for artists whose works later enter the secondary market. According to the auction house, artists 'will receive a resale royalty commission for any work purchased from Dropshop that is subsequently re-offered at Phillips – an industry first'.[40]

Including an element of on-sales protection for artists is key to other initiatives in this area. In 2022 Sotheby's created 'a new charitably-oriented primary market auction' called Artist's Choice.[41] According to Sotheby's marketing materials, this format is designed to align the interests of artists, gallerists – and presumably the auction house – and to 'empower' artists in shaping their own markets.[42] In this arrangement, the selected artists benefit from the auction house's extensive database of collectors and its reputation as a creator of markets. By leveraging this endorsement, artists enjoy the bestowal of an important prestige marker – the epithet 'collectable'. The arrangement has a novel fee structure in which an amount equal to 15 per cent of the hammer price is donated to an institution, charity or cause chosen by the artist (7.5 per cent comes out of the hammer price and this amount is matched by Sotheby's out of the premium paid by the buyer). The auction house still, therefore, receives a commission, but the remainder of the sale proceeds accrues to the relevant artist and gallerist.

In 2022 Simon de Pury also launched a series of online exhibitions and primary market auctions: 'For the first time it will be the artists themselves, and the galleries who represent them, who will receive the proceeds from an auction of works that appear for the first time on the market'.[43] According to the auction terms, 100 per cent of the hammer price is paid to the artist and gallerist; the buyer pays a premium to the auction house of 18 per cent on top of the hammer price; and 3 per cent of that premium is given to a charity. In an important measure designed to help artists develop a stable market for their works, the identities of bidders are disclosed to the artist, and buyers agree not to resell their works via auction for a three-year period.[44]

Keeping gallerists in the loop (in terms of both representation and reward) as part of a venture into the primary market eases tensions between the guardians of two traditionally distinct market sectors. Yet, Simon de Pury points out that gallerists derive important benefits from this kind of collaboration.[45] It is not merely the case that an artist on a gallerist's roster receives an advertising boost or that artists are protected from short-term flipping of their works on the secondary market. Rather, important information is shared by the auction business, including sales prices as well as the identities of purchasers and underbidders. For this reason, De Pury conceives of his new ventures into the primary market not as an 'encroachment' on the terrain of gallerists, but rather as 'significant help and enlargement' of the latter's purview. All parties are, as he puts it, operating in a single 'ecosystem', and enhanced cooperation helps the system to flourish for the benefit of everyone. This leads him to wonder why some of the world largest gallerists have not started running their own auctions? Perhaps we will see this in the coming years. For the moment, it is not simply the case that boundaries between traditional art-market segments are becoming blurred. Rather, auction houses are propelling major structural changes that are likely to have lasting effects on the market opportunities available to artists, collectors and gallerists alike.

# 3

# Creating Value

Auctions need captivating protagonists if they are to generate spectacle and value in art worlds. Typically, private passions and personal histories take the spotlight in events that are built around the holdings amassed by individuals and couples. In such cases, auction houses reinforce the notoriety of collectors as much as they promote the creativity of the artists whose works are offered for sale. Sotheby's auction of art owned by New York real-estate developers Harry Macklowe and Linda Macklowe in the spring of 2022 became the then highest grossing auction sale of all time when US$922.2 million was returned across two events. Yet, art and money competed with gossip about the Macklowes' divorce in news reports that circulated before and after the auction.[1]

Christie's branded the late Microsoft co-founder Paul G. Allen a 'visionary' for the depth and quality of the works offered in the posthumous sales of his art collection in 2022–3. A mere six months after the Macklowe sale, a new auction record was set when the Allen collection achieved returns that exceeded US$1.5 billion. Throughout the publicity material, Allen's business acumen and contributions to technological innovation were connected to his connoisseurship and capacity for taste-making. Here, as in the Macklowe case, the personal history of the collector was key to promoting the cultural significance of the works on sale.

According to Boltanski and Esquerre, narratives that focus on traditions, genealogies, identities and pedigrees constitute an 'exploitation' of the past for economic purposes.[2] Nowhere is reliance on the past as a value marker more visible than in the art market. Auction sales literature of necessity provides details about the ownership history or 'provenance' of artworks, but this communicates more than a trail of legal title. Lustre attaches to owning an object that was once part of a well-known collection or that passed through the hands of a particular individual. Stories of *where* objects have been displayed (both physically and in print) contribute to their lustre – and price. Potential buyers are always alert to the kind of company kept by the artworks that seize their imagination, and auction houses are ready to exploit each piece's social biography throughout their promotional material.

Auction catalogues are key documents in the creation of artwork 'pedigree'. These documents have evolved from simple lists of works and artists to become complex digital artefacts in which information about lots is communicated through text, film and visual comparisons with other artworks. According to Dirk Boll, this is an area that has witnessed significant developments over the past decade. From sophisticated research and due diligence to provenance study, catalogue design and, indeed, the physical and virtual exhibition of artworks, auction houses are now creating eye-catching and sophisticated presentations that appeal as much to general audiences as they do to collectors.[3]

### Bidding Mania

Art collectors who regularly frequent auctions often perform private pre-sales rituals. For those who attend in person, this may take the form of returning to a favourite chair in the auction room, dining at a special restaurant on a sales evening or sporting a particular outfit. Successful bidding requires not just financial means, a competitive spirit and a good eye. It also requires luck. Telephone bidders return to a preferred auction-house specialist, and those who employ personal advisors have close relationships to particular individuals. The factors that influence bidders beyond the tactics of the auction house itself have been objects of study in a range of disciplines.



The German psychoanalyst and collector of African art, Werner Muensterberger, devoted a book to the passion of collecting and the emotions that auctions can unleash in the acquisitive individual.[4] In terms befitting the drama of the psychoanalytic tradition, Muensterberger described the 'contagion of the frenzy and direct challenge of competition' that develops in the auction room and the 'unconscious cravings for possession, triumph and trophy-gathering' that are released in the bidder.[5] Like Boltanski and Esquerre, Muensterberger notes the attraction of acquiring objects that have 'pedigree' by virtue of their ownership history. Yet he also points to the abrupt emotional decompression that can follow the act of winning in competitive auctions. He describes the fate of one such collector: 'The event itself ended pitiably. Later, at home with his booty, the collector started to cry and shudder like a helpless young boy, confused and guilt-ridden, full of self-reproach, angst and torment. It was a kind of ex-post-facto self-punishment.'[6] While Muensterberger focuses on the cathartic release of winning an auction, economists take a more mundane approach when they pose the question: 'I have won the auction, but have I overpaid for my prize?'

Richard H. Thaler has reviewed empirical evidence of auction behaviour (though not specifically of art auctions) which suggests that the average bid in auctions is significantly less than the financial value of the relevant object.[7] This is because bidders are essentially risk averse. Paradoxically, however, the winning bid typically exceeds the value of the object. Thaler describes this as the 'winner's curse'.[8] The person who pays the highest increment bid ends up overpaying for the artefact. When bidding increments move in tens of thousands (or more), the impact of this 'curse' on the winner's pocket can be considerable.[9]

This view challenges the idea that auctions culminate in a consensual view about the value of an object that is difficult to price. Instead, it suggests that the 'winner' is, in some measure, duped by the very format of the auction, even though they are successful. The problem is exacerbated as more bidders join the fray. According to Thaler: 'An increase in the number of other bidders implies that to win the auction you must bid more aggressively, but their presence also increases the chance that if you win, you will have overestimated the value of the object for sale – suggesting that you should bid less aggressively.'[10] This idea can influence the shape of art auctions because it incentivises auction houses to place a low estimate on works offered for sale – despite pressure from consignors. The lower the estimate, the more bidders are encouraged to participate, and the more intense is the ensuing bidding war that drives up prices.[11] Perhaps the tears shed by the winner in Muensterberger's example arose less from the workings of the unconscious and more from acute awareness of having overpaid for the desired object.

Economists have not limited themselves to pointing out price problems that arise in auctions. They have also explored potential solutions. One such possibility is the 'sealed bid second-price' or 'Vickrey auction'. This format was popular among stamp collectors in the 18th and 19th centuries, but was not modelled mathematically until the 1960s by the Canadian American economist William Spencer Vickrey. The idea behind this kind of auction is that bidders will be encouraged to bid truthfully (i.e. they will be motivated to bid what they consider to be the maximum value of the lot) because if they win, they only pay the second-highest bid value (or one increment above that bid). According to Vickrey, this mechanism introduces fairness for the benefit of both buyer and seller.[12]

Vickrey auctions are not part of the mainstream art market, though variations of them feature in some online formats. On Artsy, for example, when a participant submits a maximum offer, an algorithm places bids automatically in step with pre-determined increments to maintain that individual's position as the highest bidder. If the bidder is successful, they only pay their highest bid attained at the close of the sale (subject to any further fees) – an amount that might be lower than the maximum they had been willing to pay at the outset of the auction.

In principle, because English auctions operate with verbal, ascending bids, the impact of the winner's curse is reduced. This is because participants observe patterns of bidding and can outbid their closest competitor without necessarily bidding up to their own maximum. Yet it is not always easy to achieve this transparency. In 1968 the famous American collector Norton Simon competed for a painting by Pierre-Auguste Renoir, *The Pont des Arts, Paris* (1867–8), at an auction at what was then Parke–Bernet (later merged into Sotheby's). The bidder acting on behalf of Simon stopped bidding at US$1 million to make it appear that his client's limit had been reached. According to Suzanne Muchnic, Simon then secretly took over the bidding himself, signalling instructions from behind a curtain to Peter Wilson (later of Sotheby's fame) who relayed bids to the auctioneer.[13]

The successful execution of an auction strategy may help to secure a work for a bidder, but English auctions also work in favour of the house: competition drives up the price, and the higher the winning bid, the greater the fees paid to the auction house. Studies suggest that auctioneers play an important role in this process and that much depends on their ability to generate excitement and fast-paced bidding wars.[14] From the perspective of the psychoanalyst and the economist, therefore, being a successful buyer in an English auction is a bitter-sweet prospect because winners never quite get what they pay for. But that is not the end of the story. The sociologist also has something to say on the matter.

In his *Theory of the Leisure Class* published in 1899, Thorstein Veblen used the example of Gilded Age wealth to propose that the consumption of 'excellent goods' such as artworks was a means of signalling one's reputability to other persons 'of leisure'.[15] For Veblen, it was not simply the act of consumption that was important, but rather the need for that act to be *seen* by others. He described this as 'conspicuous wastefulness', something that is 'present as a constraining norm selectively shaping and sustaining our sense of what is beautiful, and guiding our discrimination with respect to what may legitimately be approved as beautiful and what may not'.[16] Taking up Veblen's logic, the act of winning publicly in an ascending-bid auction is not just a statement about one's taste or ability to propel the circulation of highly prized objects. Having the resources to overpay at auction – and being seen to overpay – may well be part of the point.

#### Going It Alone

In the examples discussed so far, auctions have functioned as spaces that are controlled primarily by institutions. I noted in connection with digital environments that some artists have, however, also ventured directly into the marketplace by organising auctions of their own works. Why struggle to attain gallery representation when one could bring works to market independently? The logic of cutting out the intermediary seems simple, but positive outcomes are by no means guaranteed. Online auctions may offer artists a discreet way of attracting buyers because the price achieved (including whether the work sells) does not necessarily become public. But this has not always been the case.

The disastrous auction of Impressionist paintings led by Pierre-Auguste Renoir in 1875 at the Hôtel Drouot in Paris is a case in point. In holding an auction of their own works, Renoir, Claude Monet, Berthe Morisot and Alfred Sisley followed a model that had been set by Barbizon landscape painters Théodore Rousseau and Narcisse-Virgile Diaz de la Peña. The latter were keen students of the French art market and had successfully staged auctions of their own works from the middle of the 19th century to the late 1860s. Simon Kelly notes that the artist-led auction was a successful strategy for these artists because it enabled them to exploit public enthusiasm for landscape painting without having to rely on the mediation of a dealer.[17]

Renoir and his Impressionist colleagues did not fare as well when they attempted to follow this precedent. Impressionism was, at the time, still a relatively a new genre. In 1879 – only three years after this direct foray into the market – the so-called 'Independent' artists were satirised in the popular press as bohemians, revolutionaries and house painters.[18] The auction floor offered a forum for public expression of such moral and aesthetic judgements. Faced with hostilities that allegedly degenerated into the vigorous barracking of individual lots, Renoir, Monet and Morisot (and their dealer, Paul Durand-Ruel) bought back many of the works that had been offered for sale.[19]

In 2008 the British artist Damien Hirst tried his luck with this artist-led format at a Sotheby's sale titled 'Beautiful Inside My Head Forever'. On the eve of global financial crisis, Hirst's much-hyped two-day London auction featured 223 new works, including a sculpture of a golden calf made of 18 carat gold and supported by a Carrara marble plinth. Here was an artwork that proclaimed its status as a golden idol as it performed twinned aesthetic and financial values on the salesroom floor. The sale allegedly netted £111 million and broke the then record for a single-artist auction. In terms reminiscent of the Goldschmidt sale discussed in Chapter 1, *The New York Times* declared: 'The street was filled with television camera crews; fans hoping to spot celebrities like Bianca Jagger; and a crowd of collectors, dealers and curiosity seekers waiting for the doors to open. Inside later it was standing room only.'[20] The auction house may be a stage for confrontation between bidders, but it is also a competition with history.

Although Hirst's auction made headlines, it did not mark the end of the artist's engagement with gallerists – a point that signals the increasingly networked power relations of the contemporary art world. Not only had some gallerists (including Jay Jopling from London's White Cube) participated in the Sotheby's sale, but Hirst continued to be represented by gallerists including Blain Southern (closed in 2020), White Cube and Gagosian.[21] This complex of ideas was further developed in 2023 when Phillips held an exhibition of new works by Hirst in a show titled *Where the Land Meets the Sea*. In this case, Phillips acted primarily as host, using its gallery space at 30 Berkeley Square in London to introduce Hirst's latest body of work to the public. The art business service HENI managed sales, casting the event as an 'application based drop' and inviting interested parties to apply to acquire works via its website.[22] These examples from 2008 to 2023 demonstrate one artist's strategic navigation of a changing art-market infrastructure in which auction houses are extending both their functions and spheres of influence.

## Data as Spectacle

Running throughout this chapter are tensions between auctions as sites for the display and exchange of art, the promotion of new art categories and the introduction of new artists and artworks to the market. While discrepancies between aesthetic and financial value have long beset art worlds, the connection between art and global finance has become more pointed in recent decades. This reinforces a particular kind of art-market spectacle: money. Wolfgang Ullrich noted in 2009 that the media discusses art 'almost exclusively in terms of money' with the result that prices achieved at public sales have replaced interest in art's capacity to challenge and surprise audiences.[23] Less than five years later, David Joselit described art as an 'international currency' that crosses borders via art fairs, blue-chip galleries and large auction houses.[24] This tendency to think of art in increasingly financial terms has been bolstered not just by the rapid rise of art as an asset class, but – as Ullrich points out – by the languages for discussing and reporting on art transactions.

These issues are exacerbated by the proliferation of data about art that is sold at auction. Price information relating to public sales is easy to access on the internet, and a range of bespoke firms collate, package, analyse and disseminate this data. For ArtTactic, Artprice, the Sotheby's Mei Moses Indices, Artsy and Blouin Art Sales, to name just a few, price data is big business. If auctions can operate as 'validating institutions' in art worlds (see Chapter 2), do they play into the logic that conflates financial and aesthetic value by contributing to this data spectacle? If so, does it matter?

Scholars have argued that prices are cultural entities and that they illuminate social interactions and cultural rituals as they circulate.[25] This suggests that auctions are not just spaces for the transaction of art, but also for the creation of a wider range of mobile, cultural artefacts. Yet the ways in which price data is used to create rankings of artists and artworks contributes not just to a story of finance, but also to ideas that shape the writing of art's histories. Data may be spectacular, but when woven into narratives about people it has significant cultural impact.

In her study of stardom in the creative industries, Elizabeth Currid-Halkett explores a distinctive aspect of success: 'the financial rewards of the industry are also part and parcel of the ability for the artist to become part spectacle; a person whose contribution transcends their talent . . . These producer's goods become intertwined with their personae'.[26] Auctions are arenas in which the work of art 'stars' can be monetised, and it is, therefore, in the interests of auction houses to foster the creation of artists' brands and to promote their financial value. Indeed, the artist's name is often more recognisable than any of their works and takes centre stage in the financial spectacle created by data firms.[27] Yet these businesses employ a variety of methodologies in their research and create inconsistent images of individual artistic success in what is often taken to be a global art world.[28] This has led to calls for more serious efforts to collect sales data in the aggregate and with greater transparency.[29]

One consistent feature of art-auction data, however, is the presence of gender disparity in sales, particularly at the top end of the market. Artsy estimates that in 2022 the sale of works by male artists at auction achieved a total of US$9.7 billion, whereas works by women attained just over US$1 billion.[30] ArtPrice's report for the same period shows that the top ten contemporary artists by auction lot turnover were all men.[31]

Auction houses can, of course, point out that the market is a cruel truth-teller and that – in the secondary market at least – transactions mirror biases that have shaped various histories of collecting. Countering this image, auction houses – like other institutions in the cultural sector – are keen to promote themselves as agents of positive social change. They often do so by holding events featuring artists and groups of artists who have historically been marginalised in the market. Recent examples include an auction at Christie's dedicated to art by women in 2021 and the series of Sotheby's Talks on '(Women) Artists' in 2023. Yet it remains the case that international auction houses also reinforce values that have historically attached to canonical works because this is central to their business model. Paintings by Pablo Picasso, Andy Warhol and Claude Monet dominated the 2022 auction market, and works by these artists are typically marketed as 'masterpieces' of the highest value.

Through their marketing strategies, branding, catalogue essays and interviews, auction houses influence the preferences of bidders and shape the ideas of those who watch dramas unfold around the stars of the salesroom floor. Ronit Milano sums up this aspect of market spectacle and its impact on the idea of value: 'Today's art world, and by extension the art market, is ruled by celebrities. The artworks are simply the commodities through which the brand names – of people, firms, or institutions – are created and promoted'.[32] Auction houses may be theatres of contemporary art worlds, but they are also microcosms of problems and inequalities that continue to influence cultural economies and conceptions of artistic value. Data plays a role in reinforcing the spectacular economy of art auctions, but it is never neutral. Rather, it is the raw material from which auction houses construe their own image and fashion the celebrity of the artists whose works they champion.

### For Love *and* Money?

While art markets have traditionally been divided into primary and secondary segments, auctions are often understood as either 'private value' or 'common value' models. In the former, the bidder knows the value of the work to themselves, but not its value to other bidders. For example, I may be willing to pay a disproportionately high amount for a quilt by Faith Ringgold because it completes my collection of her work, but this is a fact known only to me. In a discussion of the contrasting case – common value auctions – Paul R. Milgrom and Robert J. Weber give the example of mineral rights on a piece of land: 'the values of these mineral rights to the various bidders can be regarded as equal, but bidders may have differing estimates of common value'.[33] Artworks lie somewhere between these two cases. While the value of a work to me might remain a private matter, I might also speculate on its resale value and, hence, on its value to others (its future common value). This dual aspect of value is apparent when auctions function as sites for both art acquisition and financial investment. History offers good examples of the tensions to which this gives rise.

On 2 March 1914 a group of investors led by the French art collector and industrialist André Level and calling themselves La Peau de l'ours (the 'Bearskin') staged one of the most important events in modern auction history.[34] Having invested over a ten-year period in works by European vanguard painters, the collectors auctioned their works at the Hôtel Drouot in Paris. In the catalogue Level disingenuously suggested that the consortium was simply a group of 'friends' who had acquired works 'to decorate the walls of their homes'.[35] But this masked the commercial intentions that had motivated both the acquisitions and their subsequent sale.

The consortium had approached art collecting with a strategic aim of creating a structured financial product, thereby gambling on the common value of the artefacts. Level's scheme spread risk across a pool of 'assets' produced by artists whose public reputations were still developing (Pierre Bonnard, André Derain, Paul Gauguin, Marie Laurencin, Henri Matisse and Pablo Picasso, among others) and whose works might rise or fall in financial value at different rates and at different times. Level astutely transformed art into an asset that could be structured to reduce investor risk and maximise the chance of profit on the secondary market. By acquiring works as a consortium, that risk was further diluted across the investor group.

A report in the newspaper *Gil Blas* on 3 March 1914 declared that the rooms of the Hôtel Drouot had been too small to accommodate those who wanted to participate in, or at least witness, the sale.[36] Beyond the exhibition of ambitious art, public interest was sparked by the sums at which the works were likely to be exchanged and by the proposed spectacle of the event.[37] The arts newspaper *Comœdia* drew attention to the diversity of the audience – a mixture of gallerists, collectors, artists, poets, journalists and simply curious onlookers.[38] While many of the artists whose works were included in the sale would go on to become some of the most successful of their generation, it was the Peau de l'ours investors who garnered admiration from this auction spectacle. The sale was so successful that, in the absence of laws relating to artists' resale rights, the sellers volunteered some of their profits to the artists whose works were sold in an attempt to deflect any negative publicity.

Level and his colleagues may have bought off the artists whose works they sold, but a far tenser exchange occurred in New York in 1973 during a now legendary Sotheby's auction of works owned by Robert and Ethel Scull.[39] The taxi-fleet magnate and his wife had amassed a considerable collection of Abstract Expressionist and Pop art, including works by Jasper Johns, Franz Kline, Robert Rauschenberg and Andy Warhol. According to a reporter for *The New York Times*, the sale 'possessed as much decorum as post-game activities' at Shea Stadium in Queens.[40] Demonstrators ranging from rival cab drivers (alleging Scull 'lived off the backs of cabbies') to representatives of Women in the Arts (protesting that works by only one woman were in the sale) imbued the auction with a distinctive frisson.[41]

The sale netted US$2.2 million – at the time, a record amount for the auction of works by a single seller. Yet the auction became notorious for a clash that ensued between artist and collector when Rauschenberg accused Scull of profiting from his creative labour. The artist's painting *Thaw* (1958) was one of several works that had seen a considerable uplift in value since becoming part of the Scull collection. Having acquired the painting from the New York gallerist Leo Castelli for US$900, Scull enjoyed watching it sell for US$85,000 at auction.[42] Where, Rauschenberg asked, was his cut of the profit?

The Peau de l'ours and Scull auctions illuminate changing cultural and financial values in art worlds through the lens of auction prices. In both cases, works had been acquired at a time when the relevant artists' reputations were still being established, and auctions helped to establish those works as aesthetically valuable and financially sound. Yet these public sales also staged a clash over artists' rights to financial uplift in their own works. Scull cheerfully explained to Rauschenberg that, as a collector and seller, he had contributed to the creation of a market for the artist's works. This was true, but it did not sweeten the pill for the artist.

Art worlds approach this problem in different ways, some enacting legislation to enable artists to benefit from profits upon sale of their work (a *droit de suite*), others (including initiatives in Germany and Australia) exploring the taxation of gallerists to create welfare funds for artists.[43] Perhaps the latter tax could be extended to auction houses? Instead of donating a percentage of primary-market auction sales to charity, this amount could be paid on all sales to a collective fund to support artists, particularly during the early stages of their careers. While acts of social cooperation may bring art worlds into being, these environments are fuelled as much by the pursuit of competing interests as they are by the desire to attain common goals. Auctions make the ensuing antagonisms integral to public discourses about art.

# 4

# Exhibition Cultures and Spaces

While artworks are regularly bought and sold in a variety of commercial settings, auctions are important because they publicly highlight financial, symbolic and cultural shifts in value that artefacts undergo as they change contexts. In an essay titled 'The Cultural Biography of Things', the anthropologist Igor Kopytoff pondered the consequences of objects moving between 'intermeshed exchange spheres'.[1] As discussed here in the Introduction, an artwork that achieves a low price at auction might later be deemed 'invaluable' when acquired by a museum and integrated into its permanent collection. There is little to account for that change in value other than the social significance of the physical location in which the object finds itself.

Kopytoff stresses, however, that the spheres through which artefacts pass are by no means stable and that artworks often make 'intermittent forays into the commodity sphere, quickly followed by reentries into the closed sphere of singular "art"'.[2] Illustrating this process, he points out that museums must, for example, insure their holdings and that this necessitates attaching prices to works that are, in principle, 'priceless' because they are outside the market. For Kopytoff, the wider cultural significance of such an exercise lies in its demonstration of 'an inner compulsion to defend oneself, to others and to oneself, against the charge of "merchandising" art'.[3]

Kopytoff highlights important intuitions about the impact of context on the public's experience and, indeed, conception of art. But problems arise when the boundaries that demarcate different spheres become blurred. This is a point that affects auction houses as they evolve business models designed to support both the sale and exhibition of art. Extending Kopytoff's discussion, one might ask what happens not when objects move into new contexts, but when contexts shift around objects? The circulation of artefacts between auction house and museum is a lot less easy to track when the auction house itself starts assuming the look and function of a museum.

### New Exhibition Models

Over the past decade, auction houses have increased their efforts to present works in non-sales settings. Anticipating the Hirst exhibition discussed in the previous chapter, Phillips partnered in 2015 with The Hepworth Wakefield in the UK on an exhibition of works by the British sculptor Barbara Hepworth. Merging museum culture with the commercial sphere of the auction house, Phillips emphasised that the exhibition complemented and extended an exhibition of Hepworth's works at Tate Britain by showing art from the final decade of the artist's career.[4] In 2023 Christie's London partnered with the Emirati-based Barjeel Art Foundation to host a loan exhibition of modern Arab art. Making over 150 works available to audiences, the free exhibition put Christie's imposing showrooms to good use over the slow summer period.[5]

In a similar vein, Sotheby's has collaborated on several occasions with the Duke and Duchess of Devonshire on exhibitions (and sales) of their extensive private collection. In 2019 Sotheby's worked with the owners and Rocco Forte Hotels on an exhibition that saw selected works from the Devonshire collection travel to New York, and in 2023 the London branch of the auction house hosted an exhibition of portraits from the collection to coincide with the re-opening of London's National Portrait Gallery. Describing its 'special relationship' with Chatsworth (the historic seat of the Duke of Devonshire), the auction house boasted that it had, over a 25-year period, 'provided new and exciting opportunities for members of the public to enjoy The Devonshire Collection'.[6]

Making art available to wider publics is laudable, but auction houses typically have commercial ends in sight when developing these exhibition opportunities. While the examples mentioned above were not specifically billed as including works for sale, some of them were nevertheless oriented towards sales. Christie's, for example, ran a selling exhibition of works by Hassan Sharif and other Emirati artists alongside its show of works from the Barjeel Art Foundation. Although it was displaying works from a private collection, the auction house used this exhibition strategy as a means of stimulating consumer interest in other art from the Middle East. In a similar vein, the Sotheby's exhibitions of works from the Devonshire collection served advertising and client-building purposes as much as they provided a public service. Finally, in 2023 Bonhams held an exhibition in New York titled *Spirit of Mine: Art, Identity and Postmodernism*, which showcased 'artists whose work has been historically overlooked because of their gender, race and sexuality, including those for whom identity is a core theme of their practice'.[7] The exhibition coincided with Bonham's single-lot auction of Robert Colescott's monumental painting *1919* that thematises intertwined histories of race and personal identity in the United States. In such cases, auction houses adopt the spectacle of public museum culture, but this undoubtedly helps them to further their own commercial goals.

This merging of exchange spheres also extends to the sponsorship of public exhibitions by auction houses. In 2013 Christie's sponsored an exhibition at Houghton Hall (Norfolk, UK) of the art collection amassed by British Prime Minister Robert Walpole; 2018 saw US Heritage Auctions fund a touring exhibition organised by the Norman Rockwell Museum (*Enduring Ideals: Rockwell, Roosevelt and the Four Freedoms*); in 2019 Sotheby's was a sponsor of an exhibition of works by the contemporary German artist Albert Oehlen at the Serpentine Gallery in London, while Phillips was billed (alongside the art dealership Offer Waterman) as a lead funder of *Lucian Freud: The Self Portraits* at London's Royal Academy of Arts. In Dirk Boll's view, sponsorship of such public events is a way in which auction houses can give back to the public.[8] Such generosity is welcome, but at a time when state funding for the arts is under pressure in many countries around the world, it is worth reflecting on the kinds of institution that step into the breach to shape public exhibition cultures.

## On the Move

Complementing these developments, auction houses also benefit from public museums by exploiting the movement of people. According to Alain Quemin, hiring professionals from contemporary art centres or museums enhances the symbolic and social capital of the commercial institution.[9] Recent years have witnessed a significant migration of professionals from museums to auction houses. To mention just a few: before taking up leading positions at Sotheby's and then Christie's, Guillaume Cerutti was the CEO of the Centre Pompidou in Paris; Edward Dolman joined Phillips as CEO in 2014 having served as Chair of the Qatar Museums Authority; the former Chief Curator of Painting and Sculpture at New York's Museum of Modern Art, John Elderfield, writes promotional material for Sotheby's and Christie's; Jeffrey Deitch, gallerist and former director of the Los Angeles Museum of Contemporary Art, was a panellist in the 'show' that Christie's produced to introduce its hybrid '20th Century Evening Sale' of October 2020. Exploiting a museum connection may add lustre to auction house brands, but it also reveals something about value creation in the art world. Auction houses – like commercial galleries – use the reputational power of those with experience in the museum sector to bolster the prices of the artworks they offer for sale.[10]

This trend extends to artists themselves. In 2020 British artist Tracey Emin held an exhibition at London's Royal Academy of Arts in which her works were paired with those of an artist whom she particularly admires, Edvard Munch. This was followed by Emin's first major exhibition in the Nordic region, *Tracey Emin/Edvard Munch: The Loneliness of the Soul*, which took place in 2021–2 at the renovated Munch Museum in Oslo. Capitalising on both Emin's brand and her association with Munch (including the large-scale sculpture she had created for the Munch Museum), Sotheby's invited her in 2021 to participate in their 'Expert Voices' series of short films. Ostensibly a simple interview, the film was used to market works by Munch in one of the auction house's upcoming sales. This advertising strategy extended to Emin's participation in a panel discussion about Munch's relationship to women that coincided with another auction of his work held by Sotheby's in March 2023.

Giving a public platform to artists and hearing their views about their own and others' creative practices is a valuable contribution to the knowledge framework of any art world. Does it matter if such expertise is coopted for an institution's commercial ends in cases where the relevant artists consent to such use? Taking up Kopytoff's point, does asking such a question reveal a misplaced desire to keep the worlds of art and finance separate? Regardless of one's answer, the debate returns us to the problematic intersection of aesthetic and financial values.

In a discussion of how price is attributed to objects such as artworks that have strong symbolic (as opposed to intrinsic) values, Jens Beckert argues that quality is an 'intersubjective property that emerges from the contingent assessment of the artworks by the actors in the market and does not exist independently of it'.[11] This so-called 'market from meaning' model offers a further perspective on why auction houses cultivate ties with artists and museum curators. In a world where the attribution of price depends on subjective judgement, auction houses leverage the epistemic authority of particular speakers.[12] Something as innocuous as an interview with a contemporary artist or curator can play a powerful role in helping an auction house shape ideas about value in the minds of potential bidders.

This trend is also visible in the promotion of 'curated' auctions. 'Curate' is a verb that has seeped into speech about almost all aspects of everyday life. Travellers embark on carefully curated itineraries, music lovers curate their own playlists and consultants can be employed to curate entire 'lifestyles'. In the case of auction houses, the term is loaded because it borrows from the world of museums and combines it with celebrity culture. In 2010 Phillips (then Phillips de Pury) launched a programme it called 'Carte Blanche' in which a special guest was invited to design an auction. Emphasising the merger of cultural spheres implied by this step, Simon de Pury commented at the time that it would be 'like having a guest curator at a museum'.[13]

This curatorial model is, arguably, more important than ever. In a 2023 interview, De Pury noted a new impetus behind this curatorial model, namely, the need to 'edit' a plethora of material in a crowded cultural space.[14] While seeing art through the eyes of another is an interesting experience in itself, selective curation is needed now, he said, more than ever before. Illustrating this drive, in 2018 Artcurial partnered with the interior designer Vincent Darré to stage-manage a sale of objects that once graced Paris's Ritz Hotel; Sotheby's 2019 'Treasures from Chatsworth' was conceived by David Korins, the set designer of Broadway's successful musical *Hamilton*, while the same house's 'Contemporary Curated' of 2020 showcased both art for sale and the tastemakers behind the selection of the works – Virgil Abloh (the late CEO of Off-White and Men's Artistic Director at Louis Vuitton) and Gorden Wagener (Chief Design Officer for Daimler Group). More controversially, in 2022, star of *The Batman* and *The Twilight Saga* films, Robert Pattinson, curated an auction for Sotheby's New York – a combined curatorial and sales decision that for many commentators highlighted the ascendancy of celebrity over art in a new iteration of art-world spectacle.[15]

## Valuable and Invaluable

It is not just people who move between different cultural and economic spheres that comprise art worlds. As Kopytoff notes, artworks also migrate between sales floors and museum walls and undergo value changes in the process. The display of an artwork in a museum setting typically adds to that work's financial value. In 2017 one of David Hockney's depictions of the Grand Canyon was exhibited at Tate Britain before selling for £6 million at a Sotheby's auction in London; Amedeo Modigliani's *Nu couché* (1917) was exhibited at Tate Modern in 2018 and sold by Sotheby's for US$157.2 million six weeks after the exhibition closed.[16] Georgina Adam argues that in such cases 'museums are unwittingly acting as showrooms for works subsequently sent for sale'.[17] She tantalisingly suggests that museums should benefit from the reputational uplift they have given the works by receiving 1 per cent of the subsequent sales price. Here, as in the case of artist's resale rights, it is reasonable to ask who benefits from changes in the financial fortunes of migratory objects?

A more controversial example of the movement of artworks from museums to the market is the act of deaccessioning (removing artworks from museum collections and selling them on the market). Museums do this for various reasons ranging from the desire to diversify collections to the disposal of 'lesser' works for the purpose of supporting operating costs. Sales by museums of works from their holdings raise ethical and social issues, and it is beyond the scope of this book to discuss them in detail. While guidelines for deaccessioning differ across countries, controversies arise even in cases of compliance with the rules. Publics often feel aggrieved when an artwork that has, for years, been part of the public commons is sent to the auction block.[18] In these cases, museums rather than auction houses bear the brunt of criticism, but it is an area that shines a spotlight on cross-institutional discussions that sustain or trouble art worlds.

Art historian Nizan Shaked has argued that the public 'is the entity in the name of which an art object obtains the status of cultural patrimony or heritage . . . In this context it is never a single piece of art that is at stake, but rather the piece as it relates to the collection as a whole unit'.[19] This comment recalls a characteristic of 18th-century auctions discussed earlier, namely their propensity to break up collections and propel artefacts into new contexts. While this is part of the ordinary course in the case of personal collections, it is more significant when a piece of collective cultural capital enters the private sphere. In the latter instance, auctions highlight conflicts that go to the core of how art worlds do or do not function for the benefit of their multi-faceted publics.

## Architecture

Throughout this book, I have discussed different kinds of spectacle associated with, or generated by, art auctions. The drama begins, however, before audiences even enter the salesroom. While recent decades have witnessed the advent of spectacular new museum buildings created by so-called 'starchitects' (David Adjaye, Frank Gehry, Zaha Hadid and Renzo Piano, among others), auction houses are new rivals in this competition to reshape urban environments.

In some cases, auction houses repurpose existing spaces for their events. In February 2009 Christie's used the setting of Paris's glass-domed Grand Palais to stage a spectacular exhibition and sale of works owned by Yves Saint-Laurent and Pierre Bergé. Connecting the Seine to the Champs Élysées, the Grand Palais is a magnificent 19th-century building that mounts major monographic and thematic art exhibitions annually.[20] The Saint-Laurent/Bergé auction was flanked by exhibitions of works by Pablo Picasso, Andy Warhol and Pierre-Auguste Renoir. It is estimated that nearly 34,000 people visited the Grand Palais to view over 800 pieces from Saint-Laurent and Bergé's collection that were displayed in replica rooms of the couple's apartment on the rue de Babylone.[21] Using a building that had been created to host exhibitions in the World's Fair of 1900 and that continues to be associated with museum-quality art, Christie's mounted an extraordinary display that reinforced not just the glamour of an auction, but also the capacity of the Saint-Laurent/Bergé collection to compete in a global art arena.

Some auction houses exploit the grandeur of their own historic premises. Villa Grisebach, for example, is a beautifully restored 19th-century villa on a leafy street off the famous shopping boulevard,

Kurfürstendamm, in Berlin. Since 1986, the villa has housed the Grisebach auction house, a business founded by five German art dealers with specialisms in modern German art. Stepping into the high-ceilinged exhibition rooms of this former townhouse is an encounter with history that rivals the art on show. The house holds a range of online and in-person auctions in addition to undertaking private sales. In so doing, it also advertises the broader role of its showrooms by explaining that in periods between auctions 'our Villa becomes a sort of temporary museum. A place where a new surprise could be waiting around any corner. One that can sometimes be so dramatic as to demand a redefinition of art history.'[22] This would be a bold claim for a museum, let alone an auction house. Yet it exemplifies a trend among auction houses to fulfil multiple cultural roles and to exploit the potential of their architectural spaces.

Other auction businesses capitalise on hybrid sales spaces.[23] While Tehran Auction stages auctions in the luxurious setting of the Azadi Hotel, department stores are also proving to be important partners for some auction houses. In Seoul, Shinsegae Department Store (a shareholder in Seoul Auction) has integrated art galleries into its outlets and leverages the auction infrastructure to promote art sales. Adopting a similar strategy, in 2022 K Auction partnered with the Hyundai Seoul Department Store to mount an exhibition of over 250 works.[24] These combined sales and exhibition strategies highlight the importance of commercial networks and physical infrastructures in the creation of art worlds. By partnering with retail and hotel businesses, auction houses are simultaneously extending their reach into leisure and tourism industries while capitalising on the interest of individuals who are primed to spend.

An alternative strategy is to make a new architectural statement. In 2014 Phillips opened renovated premises in Berkeley Square, London, but the arrival of its 'Park Avenue Cube' in New York in 2021 made an even bolder intervention into the urban environment. Designed by New York-based Studio MDA, Phillips's Manhattan premises is far more than an auction sales room. Rather, it is billed by the designers as a 'new and unique auction house' that maximises the potential of flexible spaces to host exhibitions, sales, lectures and other events.[25] The repositioning of the traditional auction space could not be clearer: the new building is integrated into the city to offer 'the fine qualities of a museum and the flexibility of an art fair'.[26] Rather than simply staging auctions to coincide with art fairs, the latter are now brought within the purview of the auction house itself.

The evolution of the auction house into a cultural centre and urban landmark is best illustrated by ambitions that fuelled the creation of the Guardian Art Center in Beijing. Designed by the international architecture practice Büro Ole Scheeren, the Guardian Art Center opened in 2018 and is far more than a space for auction sales. The founder of the auction house, Chen Dongsheng, explains that the centre 'consolidates various arts sector chains from exhibition and auction to warehousing and publication, links up with various aspects of society from museum and collection organisation to artist and enthusiast, and further fosters our own art ecosystem'.[27] It is a 'one-stop arts arena' that also boasts a 120-room hotel.[28]

In many respects this combined arts offering suits the distinctive infrastructure of the Chinese art world – an environment that has seen increasing consolidation in recent years. Art commentator Kejia Wu has explored connections that have emerged between art, design, fashion and technology industries across the country, including the 2017 launches of LVMH's Espace Louis Vuitton in Beijing and Prada Group's Prada Rong Zhai in Shanghai.[29] While China's auction houses increasingly seek to internationalise, so too they are competing with the import of luxury goods industries from abroad. In this case, China Guardian's desire to become a striking arts hub supports the institution's global reputation while also providing a stronghold for the domination of competitors in the region.

## Digital Spaces and New Art Genres

Consideration of how auction houses exploit different sales and exhibition spaces should not be limited to a discussion of physical environments. The increasing use of online formats for the sale of art by auction has generated new impetus for the exhibition of, and trade in, digital art forms. As buyers are willing to view works as high-resolution jpegs or to experience them through augmented and virtual reality apps, the time has seemed right for auction houses to experiment more intensively with new digital genres and online spaces for experiencing art.

A perennial problem attaching to auctions is the fact that some kinds of art suit this sales format while others do not. It is far easier to exhibit, price and transfer sculptures and paintings, for example, than pieces of conceptual or performance art. Digital art is one genre that has historically presented problems for the art market. Displaying a computer-based work, evidencing its ownership and ensuring the ongoing viability of the piece through the maintenance and updating of hardware and software are just some of the issues that have given rise to difficulties.[30] One means of combatting this is to change the discourse about digital art and to create distinctive sales and exhibition environments for it.

In 2018 Christie's took a new step when it offered an AI-generated artwork for sale. *Portrait of Edmond de Belamy*, the brainchild of a Paris-based collective called Obvious, was created by an algorithm that had been trained on a dataset of 15,000 portraits to produce a new human likeness. When the work sold for US$432,500 (nearly 45 times its high estimate), it made auction history.[31] Since 2018, generative AI has advanced considerably, and auction houses have increased their promotion of digital art forms.

Christie's took a further step in 2020 when it offered a mixed-reality performance piece for sale. *The Life* (2019) by Marina Abramović brought an avatar of the artist into the viewer's space and featured in a successful public exhibition hosted by Christie's before going under the hammer.[32] Despite initial public enthusiasm, the work failed to reach its minimum £400,000 estimate, closing at only £287,500. Undeterred, Christie's pursued its commitment to digital artforms the following year when it helped to launch one of the most controversial genres of the 21st century: non-fungible tokens (NFTs). The sale by Christie's of a digital collage comprising 5000 images and titled *Everydays: The First 5000 Days* by Beeple (Mike Winkelmann) in March 2021 was noteworthy not just because it ushered in a novel kind of artwork, but because the launch of this genre took place in an auction context.[33]

Although the excitement about NFTs may have waned since the sale of *Everydays*, the market for NFTs has by no means disappeared. Sotheby's curates NFT sales though its Natively Digital platform and runs Sotheby's Metaverse, which is dedicated to a wider selection of digital art. Phillips has collaborated with a 'virtual human', MonoC (created by the Asian brand technology group Gusto Collective), on the production and sale of generative AI works. In keeping with this trend, Christie's launched 3.0, a site that is not merely an online sales format, but an 'on-chain' platform that brands itself as 'dedicated to exceptional digital art'.[34] Unsurprisingly, it is possible to buy art here (and, increasingly, in other auction contexts) using cryptocurrencies.

While auctions have traditionally maintained the privacy of bidders by facilitating bids via telephone, online or through representatives, Christie's 3.0 allows potential purchasers to assume different identities as they explore a virtual gallery through an avatar. This raises important questions about how publics experience and acquire art – as embodied individuals or as alternative, virtual presences. In a new style of art-world sociability, there is also the possibility of meeting with other bidders (or at least their avatars) for a drink or chat in this virtual environment. If art auctions became televisual spectacles in the first two decades of the 21st century, the marketing and sale of computer-based art forms has also transformed them into online, immersive games.

# 5

# Ethics and Deregulation

This book has debated changes in value that artworks undergo as they circulate through different social and cultural contexts. Auctions play a pivotal role in creating frameworks of value while also propelling artefacts into new public and private arenas. This leads to a broader question: What kinds of art world do auctions help to create? Whether at local or international levels, auctions promote ideas about art that is worth collecting. Complementing this point, major auction houses play a prominent role in the development of art as an international asset class.

## Packaging Art in an Era of Global Finance

The promotion of art as an asset class or as loan collateral connects to a notion of value that has been explored by Aeron Davis: 'speculative value'.[1] For Davis, this differs from the social conceptions of value that have been explored in other parts of this book because it is driven by 'speculator-exchangers' who own and operate financial market networks. In the case of art worlds, the speculative value of an artefact is equivalent to its potential exchange value. While many people who acquire artworks gamble on the future value of their acquisitions, this has structural consequences for art worlds. Importantly for the present discussion, the promotion of speculative value suggests that auction houses, like investment banks, are sites of 'capital accumulation, investment and circulation'.[2]

Illustrating this point, the biography of Pablo Picasso that Sotheby's provides on its website concludes with the sentence: 'According to Sotheby's Mei Moses, the average compound annual return for Pablo Picasso is 7.4%, with 84.7% of works increasing in value'.[3] The culminating point of the artist's biography does not concern the significance of the artist's works to histories of art, but rather the possibility of their strong financial return. The role of the auction house as a site for the creation of speculative value could hardly be clearer.

It might be argued that art has always been enmeshed with capital accumulation and that people are free to buy and dispose of cultural products for whatever reasons they choose.[4] But the question arises as to whether an artist's ability to sell well at auction – that is, to function as a sound investment option – unduly impacts the chances of an artist's work achieving wider cultural appreciation. If market indices correlate artistic success with auction results, the wider picture becomes skewed very quickly.

In a study of the careers of artists from German-speaking countries, from the start of those artists' careers to 2000, Jens Beckert and Jörg Rössel argue that auction-price data reveals the importance of specific indicators of reputation: awards and media awareness of the artist.[5] By promoting artists online and through exhibitions and events, auction houses contribute to the media profiles of artists whose works they sell in public and private sales.

These issues come to the fore in the promotion of a crucial sales category – the 'contemporary'. This is a category that has impact across geographies and, as we will see, histories. In her study of the market for African art, Patricia Banks debates the absorption of African art into an international, 'mainstream' category of the contemporary: 'When included in these sales, work by African born artists is placed in the

Western marketplace without a structural or symbolic boundary distinguishing it along geographic lines'.[6] This is not merely a matter of categorisation, but rather the creation of globally attractive products that deflect attention from the unique aesthetic of particular individuals, groups or communities.[7]

The contemporary is, however, also an area where the interests of sellers, collectors, auction houses and artists can come into conflict. To cite just one example, in 2020, Ghanaian artist Amoako Boafo spoke candidly to *artnet news* about the impact of auction sales on his creative practice. Following the artist's swift rise to international fame, many of Boafo's eye-catching figurative paintings were acquired by art speculators who purchased works and quickly re-sold – 'flipped' – them at auction for staggering profits.[8] While collector enthusiasm is welcome, the stresses coupled with the recurrent circulation of Boafo's works as investment vehicles on the secondary market led to the artist's disillusionment with both the market and his role in it: 'I don't know exactly what I have to do to stop them from selling works at auction'.[9] Boafo's comment highlights the concern of many contemporary artists whose works are drawn into short-lived speculative bubbles that are akin to 'froth' in financial market terms. As public spectacles, auctions propel market churn and make it visible to audiences. It is, therefore, noteworthy that some of the primary market ventures discussed in Chapter 4 specifically seek to limit the possibility of swift resales.

### Stretching the Contemporary

The category of the 'contemporary' suggests hunger for the new, but this can work in contrasting temporal directions. One of the most eye-catching spectacles in recent auction history was Christie's New York sale of *Salvator Mundi* for just over US$450 million in 2017. Attributed to Leonardo da Vinci, but heavily restored by conservator Dianne Modestini, the painting went 'on tour' in Hong Kong, San Francisco, London and New York prior to the auction and featured in an exhibition at London's National Gallery: *Leonardo da Vinci: Painter at the Court of*

*Milan*. Billed by the auction house as 'the greatest artistic rediscovery of the 21st century', the exhibitions of *Salvator Mundi* attracted audiences from around the world and sparked widespread debate about the extent of Leonardo's input into the work.[10]

The marketing was sensational, and the auction was breathtaking in its suspense and culminating hammer price. Important for present purposes is the point that this Renaissance painting was sold by Christie's in a post-war and contemporary art evening sale. Lots either side of the piece included a sculpture by Louise Bourgeois, a drawing by Vija Celmins, a work by Keith Haring and – without apparent irony – a silkscreen by Andy Warhol titled *Sixty Last Suppers*. The inclusion of *Salvator Mundi* in this sale signalled the auction house's confidence in the ability of the market for contemporary art to attract bidders who are both acquisitive and unfazed by high price tags. The term 'contemporary' in this context attached more to the auction and its audience than to the kind of art for sale.

The point came to the fore even more dramatically in a Christie's 20th-century evening sale of 2020. This time, the artefact was a fossil – the skeleton of a T. rex that had been found in South Dakota in the United States in 1987. Affectionately referred to as 'STAN' (after the name of its discoverer, the palaeontologist Stan Sacrison), the lot was billed as an art-world 'star'. Christie's promotional material highlighted roles played by T. rex villains in Hollywood adventure films while also forging a connection between the dinosaur, celebrity culture and contemporary art. Quoting James Hislop (Head of Christie's Science and Natural History Department), the auction house's marketing material stated: 'Archetype, movie star, pop-culture celebrity, it is fitting that STAN will make his auction debut alongside masterpieces of modern and contemporary art. *T. rex* is a brand name in a way that no other dinosaur is . . . It sits very naturally against a Picasso, a Jeff Koons or an Andy Warhol.'[11] While these comments dramatically unite art, branding and celebrity, they highlight the potency of the 'contemporary' as a sales category. Whether artists are dead or alive – or, arguably, even fossilised – auction houses devise innovative strategies for making them an essential part of the present.

## Looted and Indigenous Art

The art market is often referred to as an 'unregulated' one. It is true that there is no overarching regulatory body that monitors transactions, ensures transparency or provides a unified framework of recourse if something goes wrong. This does not, however, mean that art markets sit outside law. Auction houses must comply with legal and regulatory requirements relating to matters such as contract and money laundering, for example, and they need to attend closely to the provenance of the artefacts they sell. In some cases, however, the latter gives rise to significant problems.

Recent years have seen an increased focus on the restitution of looted art. While this has led many museums to review the provenance of objects in their holdings, auction houses have also come into the spotlight. In 2001, following urgent discussions with the Commission for Looted Art in Europe, the Austrian Dorotheum auction house withdrew two landscapes by the 18th-century artist Norbert Grund on the morning their sale by auction was scheduled to take place. The Commission made the case that the paintings had been looted by the Nazis in Holland in 1941 and that the works had found their way into a private collection in Germany. While the Commission was successful in halting the sale, further work was required to prevent the auction house from returning the works to the consignor – a practice that is typical among both auction houses and commercial gallerists.[12]

As the focus on sales of art looted by the Nazis grows more intense, some auction houses are working proactively to foster provenance research. Neumeister Auctions in Munich stresses that taking a lead on this matter is crucial to establishing legal certainty for customers, but also necessary for complying with laws on the protection of cultural property that came into effect in Germany in 2016.[13] Despite the presence of guiding principles to govern the treatment of Nazi-confiscated art – the so-called Washington Principles published in 1998 – auction house practices diverge when the provenance of a work is called into question. Not all countries have committed to upholding the Washington

Principles, and there is inconsistency between national, state and regional laws.



In 2016 the Vienna-based auction house im Kinsky attracted public attention when it proposed the sale of a work – *Portrait of a Man* (1647) by Bartholomeus van der Helst – that it described in its catalogue as having a disputed provenance.[14] According to the auction house, under Austrian law the consignor had acquired the work in good faith and was, therefore, able to pass legal title in it to a new purchaser. Reports state that the consignor had tried and failed to reach agreement with the heirs of Adolphe Schloss, the former France-based collector from whom the work had been stolen. It was not until the French Ministry of Culture intervened with a request to postpone the auction that the work was withdrawn to grant the parties time to reach an agreement.[15] In the absence of any agreement, im Kinsky offered the painting for sale a year later. Following further negative publicity, however, the consignor pulled the work a few hours before the auction was scheduled to take place.[16]

The theme of Nazi-looted art highlights the pivotal role of auction houses between private and public spheres. While contending with the issue of looting entails the careful navigation of relationships with clients, claimants, charities and even governments, it also has reputational consequences. As im Kinsky discovered, a potential sale that it claimed was within the letter of the law gave rise to considerable debate in the international art and mainstream press. Auction houses are not, however, bound to reveal the identities of those who consign works to them. Even if a work is pulled from a sale and returned to its 'owner', the heirs wishing to bring a claim may find it difficult to pursue the case.

Recent auction-house initiatives in this area revolve around education and museum relationships. In 2020 Sotheby's began a collaboration with the Louvre in Paris to assist in provenance research into works the museum had acquired between 1933 and 1945. The programme was significant because, at the time, France's code on cultural heritage classified museum holdings as 'inalienable' property. It was not until June 2023 that a new law was passed by the French National Assembly to enable public institutions to return Nazi-looted art in their collections without the need for legislation to be passed in each individual case.

Auction houses are also regularly faced with issues concerning the looting of Indigenous art. Much controversy attaches to the proposed auction of works that were 'acquired' in coercive bargains in situations of war or colonial occupation. In these cases, the laws applying to auction houses are weaker than in the case of Nazi-looted art. In 2020 the hashtag #BlackArtMatters began to circulate on social media when Christie's sold two sacred sculptures (*alusi*) that had been created by the Igbo people of Nigeria. Numerous scholars objected to the sale, arguing that the works, and others like them that remain available on the market, were stolen during the Biafran war of the late 1960s. Christie's, on the other hand, argued that there was no evidence to suggest that the works had been improperly exported from their country of origin.[17]

Perhaps more so than Nazi-looted art – which is generally easier to trace – objects such as these open questions about colonial pasts that many governments, let alone auction houses, find easier to relegate to history. It is also an area that highlights the complexity of cultural networks in which auction houses, gallerists and museums are enmeshed. Paradoxically, however, auctions have also served as a public stage for the recovery of looted art (albeit via a paid transaction). During a Sotheby's sale of works with a Benin provenance in 1980, the Nigerian museologist Ekpo Eyo purchased four of the highest-priced artefacts for repatriation to Nigeria. Discussing the significant press reporting of the event and the surprise the purchases caused, Bénédicte Savoy notes that this market intervention 'did not fit the bill of an underdeveloped petitioner from the south of the Sahara' seeking Western aid for the recovery of stolen treasures.[18]

As many communities around the world point to the unlawful removal of their cultural heritage that occurred during times of war or colonial oppression, renewed focus is trained on auction houses. While an integrated approach on the part of commercial and cultural institutions to deal transparently with works of contested heritage would be advantageous, those conversations have seen uneven development. At the very least, auction-house spectacle ignites public debates about lost and stolen heritage and the importance of restitution for the ethical flourishing of contemporary art worlds.

## Theatre Games

As public events with verbal bidding, art auctions make visible the changes of price attribution in a swiftly moving scenario. There are, however, many factors that can erode confidence in the auction process. Whether bidders are physically present, bidding by telephone or participating online, it is impossible to be certain whether they act for themselves or on behalf of someone else. This is not necessarily problematic, but it can be when bids are made with the intention to inflate a price or when bidders act (unlawfully) in concert.[19] Commercial gallerists can also introduce instability into the set-up when they bid up works by 'their' artists or buy back works that threaten to sell at a sub-optimal price.

A further act that can erode trust in the auction process is 'chandelier bidding': an auctioneer looks up to a metaphorical chandelier and 'accepts' a bid from a fictional person.[20] In such cases, the auctioneer is essentially bidding on behalf of the seller to drive up the price of the work, and such 'bids' should only be taken up to the reserve price of the work (if it has one). Technically, chandelier bidding is not illegal, though it is frowned upon. Here, as in other cases, difficulty attaches to knowing that an unethical practice is being undertaken.

Anna Bolz has explored the idea of a regulatory framework for the art market while also taking a realistic look at potential problems for its implementation.[21] She notes the key role of trust and asks whether this concept can – or should – anchor an entire economic order. Bolz makes the point that artworks might sell for many millions of dollars, but that the identities of the seller, bidders, guarantor (if any) and ultimate buyer may never be known.[22] For the parties involved this may well be the desired outcome, and trusting to a process (if not to each other) can be understood as key to achieving that outcome.

In a discussion of the governance of trading in fine art at the top level of the market, Anja Shortland and Andrew Shortland debate how trust is created in a 'tricky market' where, as a general matter, only limited public resources are allocated to art crime.[23] The answer, they suggest, is the perpetuation of an 'intricate system of norms, rules and processes' put in place by a multiplicity of private decision-makers to maintain the trust of both buyers and sellers: 'Rules are enforced in pursuit of private profit and personal prestige, thus maintaining a vibrant trade at the top of the art market that is surprisingly robust against crime'.[24] Trust, they note, is based on reputation – and reputation is underpinned by 'screening procedures' on the part of agents with specialist knowledge (whether about authenticity, value or other factors pertaining to an artwork).[25]

Once again, the art auction functions as a symbol of wider ideas about markets and the relationships that structure them. But the notion that markets can 'take care of themselves' or that sophisticated investors (in this case, art buyers) are equipped to regulate disputes in private is, at best, optimistic and, at worst, damaging to the market. Financial deregulation and the creation of investment products in uninsured 'shadow banking' systems were factors that led to the global financial crisis of 2008. It might be argued that if art markets – and, in particular, auction businesses – benefit from deregulation and rely on private dispute-resolution, so too the risks associated with art speculation increase disproportionately.

## Backstage

Closely linked to the role played by auction houses in contemporary finance is the sale of works with guarantees or irrevocable bids. In the 1970s some auction houses began issuing guarantees to potential sellers for the purpose of encouraging consignments. The guarantee meant that the seller would receive a pre-agreed price for the work and that the auction house would bear the risk of a hammer price below the amount of the guarantee and retain the unsold lot itself. Aside from encouraging sellers, upsides for the auction house included a higher commission or a division of profits if the work sold for an amount above the guarantee.

In practice, this backstage arrangement saw some spectacular losses for auction houses and, by 2009, it was clear that the model needed to be changed.[26] By 2011, guarantees were still a feature of the auction market, but risk was now passed to a third party. If the price was matched in bidding, the guarantor was released from its commitment and, as in the earlier model, received a percentage of the upside between the hammer price and the pre-agreed price. If the guaranteed amount was not reached in bidding, the guarantor was committed to purchase the work. Irrevocable bids were also introduced around this time and operated in similar fashion to guarantees, with the third party bidding to an agreed, but undisclosed level.

Although guarantees have become a staple of the auction world, they remain controversial. Georgina Adam has explored industry criticism of guarantees, including claims that they drive up prices and create informational asymmetries (the amount of the guarantee is not known to other bidders).[27] In 2023 commentator Judd Tully also explored an increasing tendency on the part of guarantors to syndicate their risk by selling sub-parts of guarantees.[28] Tully notes that while this can, in some cases, flout the fine print of arrangements between the primary guarantor and the auction house, the emergence of a secondary market in guarantees is becoming a familiar feature of the market.

The question remains whether guarantees change the role of the auction house and, indeed, of the auction. When a sale is comprised of works that are, in a sense, pre-sold, the dynamic of the auction is altered: the process of 'price revelation' is no longer based on bidding, and the auction house becomes akin to a financial intermediary. In a 2023 report published by *artnet* and Morgan Stanley, concerns were raised that as the art auction market becomes more financialised, so too it becomes increasingly opaque. In particular, the tendency of auction houses to communicate premium-inclusive prices to both the media and the public was thought to sow confusion: 'first, by making it more difficult to seamlessly compare sales results with presale estimates, as the latter omit the buyer's premium; and second, by intimating that competition for the lots in question was more active than actual bidding reflected'.[29]

In 2022 the New York City Council took a step that increased opacity relating to guarantees and pricing for auctions held within its jurisdiction. Among the new rules are provisions that auction houses no longer need to be licensed by the city, third-party guarantees do not have to be disclosed and chandelier bidding can take place beyond the minimum (reserve) price of a work.[30] The changes were an attempt to bolster business activity in a post-COVID economy, but it remains to be seen whether deregulation is a viable means of achieving this purpose.

Many auction houses offer financial services to clients, and there has been a rise in specialist art-secured loans, crowd-funded art purchasing and enthusiasm for cryptocurrencies. The merger of art and finance deploys art-auction spectacle to support the exchange of sophisticated, globally tradeable assets. While artworks may be the publicly visible side of this market, the real activity takes place in the background, behind the curtain, and beneath the surface of works that, as assets, disappear into storage to await reappearance in an unfolding chain of speculative exchange.

# Conclusion

This book has explored how auctions create, contribute to and sometimes confound art worlds. As art commerce expands, auction culture is undergoing radical change. By challenging hitherto familiar boundaries of art markets, exploiting the potential of digital technologies and forging new relationships between collectors, artists, museums and gallerists, auctions have become pivotal elements in diverse cultural and financial landscapes.

Despite their rules-based nature, auctions do not function in consistent ways. Nor are they solely the preserve of multi-national businesses. Instead, auctions are subject to different laws and guidelines depending on where they are held, sometimes appealing to local institutional frameworks and sometimes underestimating the importance of specific cultural needs. While the largest auction houses continually seek to grow their businesses across borders, others cater to regional interests and aim to support the creativity and collecting habits of local audiences. Regardless of differences in sales formats and institutional structures, auctions are a powerful lens through which to study different priorities, ambitions and assumptions that shape art worlds.

In addition to serving as spaces for the exchange of art, auctions complicate ideas about cultural value and financial worth by encouraging reflection on the ideals that motivate the evolution of different art worlds. It is not easy to balance the competing interests of emerging artists, creative 'stars', collectors, investors, gallerists, art lovers, museums and business enterprises. This task is even more difficult against a background of contemporary inequalities based on gender and race, uneven distributions of wealth and income, colonial legacies and histories of bias that continue to impact on the valuation, circulation and exhibition of art. Auctions are arenas that bring these social, economic and cultural tensions dramatically to the fore.

I hope to have shown the different roles that auctions fulfil for a range of actors. Whether or not people participate in auctions, these events drive wider changes in exhibition styles, art genres, finance and cultural marketing. Auction houses themselves are deepening their roots in different communities, metamorphosing into all-purpose arts centres and, in some cases, transforming physical and cultural landscapes. For these reasons, auctions are important – even to those who may never set foot on a salesroom floor.

The expansion of auctions and auction house businesses online has further strengthened the significance of this strand of art-world spectacle. By creating innovative opportunities for audience engagement and contributing to an emerging digital heritage, auctions drive new histories of art through the creation and dissemination of information. Yet the increasing financial and epistemic power of both large and small auction houses also poses a threat to the stability of art worlds. Institutions may explore and then back out of markets or terminate initiatives simply because it suits the demands of their changing business models.

While many new sales initiatives have altruistic ends in view, for auction houses they are also commercial strategies. From the perspective of the industry as a whole, we are witnessing an increasing convergence between large auction businesses and global luxury goods industries. Groupe Artémis (founded by François Pinault) owns Christie's, and the Russian luxury retail group Mercury owns Phillips. Demonstrating the increasing bond between the two industries, Christie's CEO Guillaume Cerutti opened a public message of January 2024 by emphasising the 'continued attraction of the art and luxury market to new buyers'.[1] He went on to note the financial significance of this appeal by explaining that 'art and luxury objects can be attractive and secure investments, particularly when other asset classes appear more volatile'.[2] Large auction houses may open new opportunities for artists, audiences and buyers, but their close connection to luxury and finance means that they are also capable of using art to entrench socioeconomic privilege. The deeper question is whether these two tendencies can be reconciled in a just art world.

Auction houses have no particular commitment to the sustainable functioning of art worlds or their markets. Nor are they under an obligation to maximise opportunities for artists. Here, as elsewhere, exploring the relational elements of art worlds highlights the different goals and strategies that private, public and state-owned entities pursue in their distinctive contributions to visual-arts landscapes. Yet many of the initiatives I have explored in this book also attest to a desire on the part of auction businesses to make a positive contribution to art communities. Balancing a degree of market scepticism on my part, Simon de Pury offered an optimistic view of the future, including the positive role that auction houses might play in creating a more open art world. He predicted that as digital technologies continue to develop, a form of 'auction play' will develop on the part of audiences. According to De Pury, this, coupled with the benefits to auction houses of technological efficiency, will lead to market growth, new opportunities for education and a democratisation of the art world.[3] I hope he is right.

For artists, auctions create both opportunities and barriers to success. For collectors, they are rituals of pleasure. For most people, they are a form of art-world theatre known mostly through books, films, television and the internet. Yet auctions – and the enterprises, communities and individuals that sustain them – are leading innovations in the promotion and sale of art. Whether one is thrilled, intrigued or simply bemused by them, auctions are poised to make a crucial contribution to the expanding theatre of 21st-century art worlds.

# Notes

## Introduction

1 See Charles W. Smith, *Auctions: The Social Construction of Value* (Berkeley: University of California Press, 1990), p.174.

2 Eileen Kinsella, 'How a $10 Million Miró Auction Flop Turned Into a Dream Come True for One Dutch Museum', *artnet news*, 29 September 2022, https://news.artnet.com/market/museum-boijmans-celebrates-miro-masterpiece-2183147. Accessed 21 July 2023.

3 Scott Reyburn, 'Five years since the $450m Salvator Mundi sale: a first-hand account of the nonsensical auction', *The Art Newspaper*, 15 November 2022, https://www.theartnewspaper.com/2022/11/15/five-years-since-the-450m-salvator-mundi-sale-a-first-hand-account-of-the-nonsensical-auction. Accessed 17 November 2023.

4 Thierry Ehrmann, Céline Moine and Jean Minguet, *The Art Market in 2022* (Paris: Artmarket.com, 2023), pp 8 and 25, https://www.artprice.com/artprice-reports/the-art-market-in-2022. Accessed 11 November 2023.

5 Phillips, Press Release, 6 July 2023, https://www.phillips.com/press/release/phillips-celebrates-david-hockney-by-establishing-an-annual-auction-dedicated-to-the-artists-work. Accessed 11 November 2023.

6 Robin Pogrebin, 'Paul G. Allen's Art at Christie's Tops $1.5 billion, Cracking

Records', *The New York Times*, 9 November 2022, https://www.nytimes.com/2022/11/09/arts/design/paul-allen-auction-christies.html. Accessed 9 November 2023.

7 Annie Armstrong, 'Sotheby's Emily Fisher Landau Sale is Most Valuable Ever for a Female Collector, Nets $406 Million', *artnet news*, 9 November 2023, https://news.artnet.com/market/emily-fisher-landau-sothebys-results-2391881. Accessed 9 November 2023. Reports also note, however, that the sales proceeds were at the lower end of the auction house estimate. See Tim Schneider, 'The art market in 2023: shaky year for heavily guaranteed single-owner sales', *The Art Newspaper*, 5 December 2023, https://www.theartnewspaper.com/2023/12/05/the-art-market-in-2023-cracks-forming-in-single-owner-sales-strategy. Accessed 11 December 2023.

8 Luc Boltanski and Arnaud Esquerre, *Enrichment: A Critique of Commodities*, translated by Catherine Porter (Cambridge: Polity, 2020), p.32.

9 ibid., p.34.

10 For further reading see Robert H. Frank and Philip J. Cook, *The Winner-Take-All-Society* (London: Virgin Books, 2010); Michael Findlay, *The Value of Art: Money, Power, Beauty*, 2nd edition (Munich: Prestel, 2022).

11 Some scholars offer an even finer distinction by identifying the secondary market with sales from gallerists to collectors and a tertiary market with auction house resales. See Leslie Singer and Gary Lynch, 'Public Choice in the Tertiary Art Market', *Journal of Cultural Economics*, vol.18, 1994, pp 199–216.

12 See Michael Shnayerson, *Boom: Mad Money, Mega Dealers, and the Rise of Contemporary Art* (New York: Public Affairs, 2019, p.202); Simon de Pury, 'Auction Houses Are Shifting More and More to Private Sales', 26 January 2021, *artnet news*, https://news.artnet.com/art-world/private-sales-auction-houses-galleries-1939075. Accessed 27 November 2023.

13 Howard S. Becker, *Art Worlds*, 2nd edition (Berkeley: University of California Press, 2008), p.35.

14 ibid.

### 1: Auction as Spectacle

1 See https://www.auktionsverket.com/en/our-history/. Accessed 11 December 2023.

2 See https://www.dorotheum.com/en/c/the-company-28/. Accessed 11 December 2023.

3 The Getty Provenance Index lists the earliest surviving British art catalogue as the posthumous sale of the collection of the painter Sir Peter Lely in 1682. https://www.getty.edu/research/tools/provenance/index.html. See also Brian Learmount, *A History of the Auction from 500 BC to the Present Day* (Market Harborough: The Book Guild Ltd, 2021).
4 John Michael Montias, *Art at Auction in 17th Century Amsterdam* (Amsterdam: Amsterdam University Press, 2002), p.11.
5 See https://www.freemansauction.com/about-us. Accessed 11 December 2023.
6 Shireen Huda, *Pedigree and Panache: A History of the Art Auction in Australia* (Canberra: Australian National University, 2008), p.37.
7 This landmark sale was an international media event, attracted overseas buyers and achieved a total sale price of US$2.7 million. See ibid., p.114.
8 See Ralph Cassady Jr, *Auctions and Auctioneering* (Berkeley: University of California Press, 2021).
9 Cynthia Wall, 'The English Auction: Narratives of Dismantlings', *Eighteenth-Century Studies*, vol.31, no.1, 1997, pp 1–25, p.20.
10 ibid., p.5.
11 John Ott, 'How New York Stole the Luxury Art Market: Blockbuster Auctions and Bourgeois Identity in Gilded Age America', *Winterthur Portfolio*, vol.42, nos 2–3, 2008, pp 133–58, p.136.
12 Philip Hook, *Rogues' Gallery: A History of Art and its Dealers* (London: Profile Books, 2017), p.207.
13 'Peter Wilson, Sotheby's Sublime Auctioneer', *Vogue*, June 1962, p.118. See also Cassady, *Auctions and Auctioneering*, pp 103–4.
14 See Hook, *Rogues' Gallery*, pp 215–17.
15 The Museum of Modern Art, New York, held an exhibition of paintings from Robinson's collection from 4 March–12 April 1953.
16 *The Sphere*, vol.235, issue 3056, 25 October 1958, pp 144–5.
17 *The Illustrated London News*, 25 October 1958, p.1.
18 Clare McAndrew, *The Art Market 2021* (Basel: Art Basel and UBS, 2021), pp 230–31.
19 Christine Bourron (CEO of Pi-eX Ltd), 'How Has Covid-19 Affected the Public Auction Market', *Arts*, vol.10, no.74, 2021, pp 1–23, p.3.
20 For further detail of the prices achieved in online-only auctions during this period, see ibid., p.10.
21 Sotheby's, 'Record-Breaking Rembrandt to Richter Sale Reinvents the Auction', 29 July 2020, https://www.sothebys.com/en/articles/record-

breaking-rembrandt-to-richter-sale-reinvents-the-auction. Accessed 16 February 2023. For further discussion see Kathryn Brown, 'Screen Culture, Online Auctions, and Art Market Spectacle', *Visual Studies*, vol.38, nos 3–4, 2023, pp 377–88.

22 Dirk Boll, 'A Cultural History of the Art Auction in 14 Portraits', in *Auctioneers Who Made Art History* , ed. Dirk Boll (Berlin: Hatje Cantz, 2020), pp 6–13, p.9.

23 Sotheby's Press Release, 30 June 2020, 'Sotheby's Live Global Auction Event Achieves $363.2 Million And 93% Sold', Sothebys.com. Accessed 10 November 2023.

24 Scott Reyburn, 'Art Auction or Game Show? Sotheby's Tries Something New', *The New York Times*, 15 July 2020, nytimes.com/2020/06/30/arts/design/sothebys-online-auction.html. Accessed 24 August 2023.

25 Jonathan Bastable, '"Welcome to the new theatre": The four auctioneers – all for *ONE*', Christie's.com, 3 July 2020, https://www.christies.com/features/All-for-ONE-The-four-auctioneers-10757-1.aspx?sc_lang=en#FID-10757. Accessed 16 February 2023.

26 'If People Can't Come to Us, We'll Create An Exciting Product and Take it Into Their Homes', Christie's.com, https://www.christies.com/features/Christies-new-PWC-format-in-New-York-11005-3.aspx. Accessed 16 February 2023.

27 Boltanski and Esquerre, *Enrichment*, p.32.

28 Sotheby's, 'Record-Breaking Rembrandt to Richter Sale Reinvents the Auction'.

29 Clare McAndrew, *A Survey of Global Collecting in 2022* (Basel: Art Basel and UBS, 2022), p.18.

30 Christie's, 'Wrap report: Iconic Giacometti crowns €118.1 million sale of Givenchy collection in Paris', 30 June 2022, https://www.christies.com/en/stories/iconic-giacometti-crowns-83-million-euro-givenchy-sales-74caad682fa84ba4b46ca034b638bf36?lid=1. Accessed 9 November 2023.

31 The French Auction Market Authority (Conseil des ventes volontaires), *The Latest Trends in the Art Market: France and International Auction Sales* (Paris: Beaux Arts & Cie, 2022), pp 13, 16

32 Clare McAndrew, *The Art Market 2023* (Basel: UBS and Art Basel, 2023), p.163.

33 See the auction house's website, https://www.seoulauction.com/footer/companyIntro. Accessed 13 July 2023.

34 See the description on Singulart's website, https://www.singulart.com/en/events/auctions. Accessed 25 July 2023.

35 Smith, *Auctions*, pp 17–18.

36 For further detail see https://theauctioncollective.com/the-auction-collective-story/. Accessed 31 July 2023.

37 Ans Azura website, https://ansazura.com/en/about-us. Accessed 17 July 2023.

### 2: Expanding Markets

1 McAndrew, *The Art Market 2023*, p.139.

2 Leili Sreberny-Mohammadi, 'The Emergence of an Auction Category: Iranian Art at Christie's Dubai, 2006–2016', *Arts*, vol.10, no.35, 2021, https://doi.org/10.3390/arts 10020035, p.15.

3 ibid.

4 Larissa Buchholz, *The Global Rules of Art* (Princeton: Princeton University Press, 2022), p.84.

5 Rozita Sharafjahan, Anahita Ghabaian, Maryam Majd, Masoumeh Mozaffari, Combiz Moussavi-Aghdam and Keivan Moussavi-Aghdam, 'In Tehran: A Conversation with Iranian Gallerists', *Art Journal*, vol.77, no.4, 2018, pp 6–25, p.7.

6 Michelle Moghtader, 'Iran's domestic art scene thrives despite economic sanctions', *Reuters*, 1 June 2014, https://www.reuters.com/article/idUSL6N0OF0UW/. Accessed 11 December 2023.

7 Interview with the author, 29 November 2023.

8 Tehran Auction's website contains details of its mission and sales history, https://tehranauction.com/en/about-us/. Accessed 21 July 2023.

9 Najmeh Bozorgmehr, 'Iran gets a piece of the auction', *The Financial Times*, 27 June 2012, https://www.ft.com/content/0fbd798a-bec4-11e1-8ccd-00144feabdc0. Accessed 21 July 2023.

10 Moghtader, 'Iran's domestic art scene thrives despite economic sanctions'.

11 Saeed Kamali Dehghan, 'Tehran auction shifts millions of pounds worth of art in spite of sanctions', *The Guardian*, 1 June 2015, https://www.theguardian.com/world/2015/jun/01/tehran-auction-sells-millions-pounds-art-despite-iran-sanctions. Accessed 11 December 2023.

12 Moghtader, 'Iran's domestic art scene thrives despite economic sanctions'.

13 On the impact of economic sanctions see Ahmad Rafiei Vardanjani, 'United States Economic Sanctions on Iran and Their Impacts on the

Middle Eastern Art Market', *Arts*, vol.9, no.4, 2020, https://doi.org/10.3390/arts9040132, p.132.

14 Filip Vermeylen, 'The India Art Fair and the Market for Visual Arts in the Global South', in *Cosmopolitan Canvases: The Globalization of Markets for Contemporary Art*, eds Olav Velthuis and Stefano Baia Curioni (Oxford: Oxford University Press, 2015), pp 31–54, p.32.

15 Olga Kanzaki Sooudi, 'Making Mumbai's Emerging Art World through Makeshift Practices', *Journal of South Asian Studies*, vol.39, no.1, 2016, pp 149–66, p.165.

16 Data suggests that the Indian auction market continues to rise with a 9 per cent increase in turnover (total US$144.3 million) and a 6 per cent increase in the number of works sold (3833) over 2022–3. Indian Art Investor and Grant Thornton Bharat, *State of the Indian Art Market Report FY 23*, p.8 as reported in https://www.grantthornton.in/press-room/indian-art-market-witnesses-a-successful-year-with-a-turnover-of-usd-144.3-million-in-fy-2023/. Accessed 12 March 2024. Olga Kanzaki Sooudi, 'From Mumbai to London: Co-Constituting Value in Art from India via Local and Global Circuits of Exchange', in *Global Art in Local Artworlds: Changing Hierarchies of Value*, eds O. Salemink, A. Siegel Corrêa, J. Sejrup and V. Nielsen (Abingdon: Routledge, 2023), pp 193–217.

17 Jonathan Adeyemi, *Contemporary Art from Nigeria in the Global Markets: Trending in the Margins* (Cham: Palgrave Macmillan, 2022), p.95.

18 ibid., p.11.

19 'Freeman's Presents "Reflections" with Navanjali Kelsey and Hong-Bich Huynh Vernon', 19 July 2022, https://www.pafa.org/news/freemans-presents-reflections-navanjali-kelsey-hong-bich-huynh-vernon-071922. Accessed 13 February 2024.

20 Arsalan Mohammad, 'Sotheby's Partners with Saudi Arabia's Inaugural Islamic Art Biennale', 16 January 2023, https://www.sothebys.com/en/articles/sothebys-partners-with-saudi-arabias-inaugural-islamic-arts-biennale. Accessed 20 November 2023.

21 Freeman's | Hindman, 'About Us', https://www.freemansauction.com/about-us. Accessed 13 February 2024.

22 Alain Quemin, *Le Monde des galeries: Art contemporain, structure du marché et internationalisation* (Paris: CNRS Editions, 2021), p.134.

23 Georgina Adam, 'Are art fairs big enough for both galleries and auction

houses?', *The Art Newspaper*, 1 November 2011, https://www.theartnewspaper.com/2011/11/01/are-fairs-big-enough-for-both-galleries-and-auction-houses. Accessed 17 November 2023.

24 Bolsa de Arte, 'About us', https://www.bolsadearte.com/a-empresa/sobre-nos/. Accessed 25 July 2023.

25 Fresh Art Fair's webpage, https://www.freshartfair.net/bonhams-auctioneers/. Accessed 31 July 2023.

26 See https://www.1-54.com/london/. Accessed 30 November 2023.

27 Kabir Jhala, 'Art and Bollywood go off to the races: Mumbai to get its first major art fair this November', *The Art Newspaper*, 31 July 2023, https://www.theartnewspaper.com/2023/07/31/art-meets-bollywood-at-the-races-mumbai-to-get-first-major-art-fair-this-november. Accessed 1 August 2023.

28 See, for example, Tim Schneider, 'Auctioneers are Gatecrashing the Primary Market. But That Might Not Be a Terrible Thing', *artnet news*, 21 September 2022, https://news.artnet.com/market/gray-market-zero-base-sothebys-artists-choice-2179226. Accessed 19 November 2023.

29 Svetlana Kharchenkova and Olav Velthuis, 'How to become a Judgment Device: Valuation Practices and the Role of Auctions in the Emerging Chinese Market', *Socio-Economic Review*, vol.16, no.3, 2018, pp 459–77, p.465.

30 ibid., p.472.

31 Interview with the author, 7 December 2023.

32 On recent changes to museum culture in China see Xianyuan Chang, Zhaoping Wu, Yi Chen, Yuanyuan Du, Longfei Shang, Ying Ge, Jie Chang and Guofu Yang, 'The Booming Number of Museums and their Inequality Changes in China', *Sustainability*, 2021, vol.13, no.24, article 13860, pp 1–19.

33 William Langley, 'China's largest auction houses plan to take on western rivals', *The Financial Times*, 30 April 2023, https://www.ft.com/content/e3e8e80a-8ded-494b-a1d0-eb978c34b492. Accessed 8 December 2023.

34 See Aimee Dawson, 'Does coverage of Sotheby's Freddie Mercury sales show that auctions are perfect TikTok fodder?', *The Art Newspaper*, 4 October 2023, https://www.theartnewspaper.com/2023/10/04/does-coverage-of-sothebys-freddie-mercury-sales-show-that-auctions-are-perfect-tiktok-fodder. Accessed 8 December 2023.

35 Rosa Escadon, 'TikTok expands into e-commerce with TikTok Shop', *Forbes*, 14 September 2023, https://www.forbes.com/sites/rosaescandon/2023/09/14/tiktok-expands-into-e-commerce-with-tiktok-shop/. Accessed 8 December 2023.

36 See the auction house's press release, 'An Eye For the Future', https://www.seoulauction.com/nas_img/front/homepage/20220831_seoulauction_E.pdf. Accessed 19 November 2023.

37 Christian Davies, 'Galleries and auction houses at loggerheads in Seoul', *The Financial Times*, 26 August 2022, https://www.ft.com/content/4bd82da6-ccb9-4376-b649-e94626272a5e. Accessed 27 July 2023.

38 Park Han-Sol, 'Auction houses, galleries dip their toes into each other's territory', *The Korea Times*, 3 September 2022, https://www.koreatimes.co.kr/www/art/2023/07/398_325197.html. Accessed 27 July 2023.

39 See Phillips's website for further details, https://dropshop.phillips.com/pages/about; Phillips press release 7 August 2023, https://www.phillips.com/press/release/phillips-announces-groundbreaking-new-digital-platform-presenting-works-by-contemporary-artists-and-makers; Anny Shaw, 'Phillips launches Dropshop, selling newly commissioned works direct from artist to collector', *The Art Newspaper*, 8 August 2023, https://www.theartnewspaper.com/2023/08/08/phillips-launches-dropshop-selling-newly-commissioned-works-direct-from-artists-to-collector. Accessed 16 November 2023.

40 Phillips, press release, 7 August 2023.

41 For further detail see Sotheby's webpage, https://www.sothebys.com/en/series/artists-choice. Accessed 27 July 2023.

42 ibid.

43 Details are on Simon de Pury's website, https://auction.de-pury.com/en/auction/005-women-art-in-times-of-chaos#. Accessed 14 August 2023.

44 Art Daily, https://artdaily.cc/news/147881/Simon-de-Pury-announces-a-new-series-of-curated-auctions. Accessed 27 July 2023.

45 Interview with the author, 27 November 2023.

### 3: Creating Value

1 Henry Samuel, 'Bitter $2bn divorce spawns the most expensive art auction ever', *The Telegraph*, 17 May 2022, https://www.telegraph.co.uk/world-news/2022/05/17/harry-macklowe-art-collection-bitter-divorce-spawns-sothebys-auction/; Scott Reyburn and Robin Pogrebin, 'The Macklowe Collection Tops $922 Million at Auction', *The New York Times*, 6 May 2022, https://www.nytimes.com/2022/05/16/arts/design/macklowe-collectors-sothebys-art-warhol-richter.html. Accessed 14 August 2023.

2 Boltanski and Esquerre, *Enrichment,* pp 113, 179 and 303.

3 Interview with the author, 29 November 2023.

4 Werner Muensterberger, *Collecting: An Unruly Passion: Psychological Perspectives* (Princeton: Princeton University Press, 1994).

5 ibid., pp 245–6.

6 ibid., p.247.

7 Richard H. Thaler, 'Anomalies: The Winner's Curse', *Journal of Economic Perspectives*, vol.2, no.1, 1988, pp 191–202.

8 ibid., p.192.

9 See also Christian Heath, *The Dynamics of Auction: Social Interaction and the Sale of Fine Art and Antiquities* (Cambridge: Cambridge University Press, 2014), p.198.

10 Thaler, 'Anomalies', p.192.

11 Robert B. Ecklund Jr, John D. Jackson and Robert D. Tollison, *The Economics of American Art: Issues, Artists, and Market Institutions* (Oxford: Oxford University Press, 2017), p.119. See also Don Thompson, *The Orange Balloon Dog: Bubbles, Turmoil and Avarice in the Contemporary Art Market* (London: Aurum Press, 2018), p.202.

12 William Vickrey, 'Counterspeculation, Auctions, and Competitive Sealed Tenders', *The Journal of Finance*, vol.16, no.1, 1961, pp 8–37.

13 Suzanne Muchnic, *Odd Man In: Norton Simon and the Pursuit of Culture* (Berkeley: University of California Press, 1998), p.63.

14 Nicola Lacetera, Bradley J. Larsen, Devin G. Pope and Justin R. Sydnor, 'Bid Takers or Market Makers? The Effect of Auctioneers on Auction Outcome', *American Economic Journal: Microeconomics*, vol.8, no.4, 2016, pp 195–229, p.198.

15 Thorstein Veblen, *The Theory of the Leisure Class: An Economic Study of Institutions* (Oxford: Oxford University Press, 2009), p.69.

16 ibid., p.86.

17 Simon Kelly, *Théodore Rousseau and the Rise of the Modern Art Market: An Avant-Garde Painter in Nineteenth-Century France* (London: Bloomsbury, 2021), p.161.

18 Anthea Callen, 'The Female Spectator of Modern Art and the Spectacle of Medicalized Femininity', in *Perspectives on Degas*, ed. Kathryn Brown (Abingdon: Routledge, 2017), pp 73–93.

19 Merete Bodelsen, 'Early Impressionist Sales 1874–94 in the Light of Some Unpublished "Procès-Verbaux"', *The Burlington Magazine*, vol.110, no.783, 1968, pp 330–49, p.333; Frances Fowle, '"Impressionnistes" et "intransigeants":

The 1875 auction at the Hôtel Drouot and the role of Léon Monet', in *Léon Monet, Frère de l'artiste et collectionneur*, ed. Geraldine Lefebvre (Paris: Réunion des Musées nationaux, 2023), pp 86–95.

20 Carol Vogel, 'Hirst's Art Auction Attracts Plenty of Bidders, Despite Financial Turmoil', *The New York Times*, 15 September 2008, https://www.nytimes.com/2008/09/16/arts/design/16auct.html. Accessed 31 July 2023; Olav Velthuis, 'Damien's Dangerous Idea, Valuing Contemporary Art at Auction', in *The Worth of Goods: Valuation and Pricing in the Economy*, eds Jens Beckert and Patrik Aspers (Oxford: Oxford University Press, 2011), pp 178–200, p.185.

21 See Quemin, *Le Monde des galeries*, p.165.

22 See Heni press release, 26 October 2023, https://resources.heni.com/HENI%20Primary%20-%20Damien%20Hirst%20-%20Paper%20Blossoms%20Press%20Kit.pdf; Anny Shaw, 'Lines redrawn: how artists and auction houses are shaking things up with new ways of working together', *The Art Newspaper*, 16 October 2023, https://www.theartnewspaper.com/2023/10/16/lines-redrawn-how-auction-houses-are-shaking-things-up-with-new-ways-of-working-with-artists. Accessed 16 November 2023.

23 Wolfgang Ullrich, 'Icons of Capitalism: How Prices Made Art', extracts published in *The Art Market*, ed. Natasha Degen (London and Massachusetts: Whitechapel Gallery and MIT Press, 2013), pp 40–41, p.41.

24 David Joselit, *After Art* (Princeton: Princeton University Press, 2013), p.1.

25 Olav Velthuis, *Talking Prices: Symbolic Meanings of Prices on the Market for Contemporary Art* (Princeton: Princeton University Press, 2005); L. Adkins and T.-K. Lehtonen, 'Price: An Introduction', *Distinktion: Journal of Social Theory*, vol.19, no.2, 2018, pp 109–16.

26 Elizabeth Currid-Halkett, 'Stars and Stardom in the Creative Industries', in *The Oxford Book of Creative Industries*, ed. Candace Jones (Oxford: Oxford University Press, 2013), pp 171–83, pp 171–2.

27 Marketing issues relating to name recognition are debated by Anne-Sophie V. Radermecker in *Anonymous Art at Auction: The Reception of Early Flemish Paintings in the Western Art Market (1946–2015)* (Leiden: Brill, 2021).

28 Alain Quemin, 'The Superstars of Contemporary Art: A Sociological Analysis of Fame and Consecration in the Visual Arts through Indigenous Rankings of the "Top Artists in the World"', *Revista do Instituto de Estudos Brasileiros*, no.66, 2017, pp 1–16.

29 H.J. van Miegroet, K.P. Alexander and F. Leunissen, 'Imperfect Data, Art

Markets and Internet Research', *Arts*, vol.8, no.76, 2019, https://www.mdpi.com/2076-0752/8/3/76. Accessed 15 August 2023.

30 Arun Kakar and Casey Lesser, 'The State of the Market for Women Artist's Work', in *The Women Artists Market Report (Artsy)*, 8 March 2023, https://www.artsy.net/article/artsy-editorial-state-market-women-artists-work. Accessed 3 August 2023.

31 ArtPrice.com and Artron.net, *The Art Market in 2022* (Lyon and Beijing, 2023), p.50.

32 Ronit Milano, 'Moralizing the Art Market: A Socioeconomic Perspective on Art Auctions on the Floor and Online', *Journal for Art Market Studies*, vol.1, 2019, pp 1–18, p.11.

33 Paul R. Milgrom and Robert J. Weber, 'A Theory of Auctions and Competitive Bidding', *Econometrica*, vol.50, no.5, 1982, pp 1089–122, pp 1093–4.

34 For further discussion see Kathryn Brown, 'Disappearing Acts: Fictitious Capital, Aesthetic Atheism, and the Artworld', *Journal of Visual Art Practice*, vol.19, no.3, 2020, pp 225–40, doi.org/10.1080/14702029.2020.1808336.

35 André Level, *Collection de la Peau de l'ours* (Paris: Hôtel Drouot, 1914), n.p.

36 Seymour de Ricci, 'La Peau de l'ours', *Gil Blas*, 3 March 1914, p.4.

37 For further discussion see Michael Fitzgerald, *Making Modernism: Picasso and the Creation of the Market for Twentieth-Century Art* (Berkeley: University of California Press, 1995), pp 36–40.

38 André Warnod, 'La vente de la "Peau de l'Ours"', *Comœdia*, 3 March 1914, p.3.

39 Sotheby's was at the time Sotheby's Parke-Bernet.

40 Fred Ferretti, 'Scull's U.S. Art Brings Record $2 Million', *The New York Times*, 19 October 1973, p.57, https://www.nytimes.com/1973/10/19/archives/sculls-us-art-brings-record-2-million.html. Accessed 14 August 2023.

41 ibid.

42 John Henry Merryman, 'The Wrath of Robert Rauschenberg', *The American Journal of Comparative Law*, vol.41, no.1, 1993, pp 103–27, p.110.

43 These alternatives are debated in Merryman, 'The Wrath of Robert Rauschenberg'.

#### 4: Exhibition Cultures and Spaces

1 Igor Kopytoff, 'The Cultural Biography of Things: Commoditization as Process', in *The Social Life of Things: Commodities in Cultural Perspective,* ed. Arjun Appadurai (Cambridge: Cambridge University Press, 1986), pp 64–92, p.82.

2 ibid., p.83.
3 ibid., p.83.
4 Phillips, 'Barbara Hepworth: Sculpture Redefined', https://www.phillips.com/article/4329375/barbara-hepworth-sculpture-redefined. Accessed 1 August 2023.
5 Christie's, 'Kawkaba: Highlights from the Barjeel Art Foundation', July–August 2023, https://www.christies.com/en/events/special-events/kawkaba-highlights-from-the-barjeel-art-foundation/about. Accessed 1 August 2023.
6 Sotheby's, 'Portraits from Chatsworth: A Loan Exhibition', May–July 2023, https://www.sothebys.com/en/digital-catalogues/portraits-from-chatsworth. Accessed 1 August 2023.
7 Bonham's, press release, https://www.bonhams.com/press_release/36961/. Accessed 14 November 2023.
8 Interview with the author, 29 November 2023.
9 Alain Quemin, 'The Market and Museums: The Increasing Power of Collectors and Private Galleries in the Contemporary Art World', *Journal of Visual Art Practice*, vol.19, no.3, 2020, pp 211–24, p.218.
10 Raymonde Moulin, 'The Museum and the Marketplace: The Constitution of Value in Contemporary Art', translated by Michel Vale, *International Journal of Political Economy*, vol.25, no.2, 1995, pp 33–62, p.33.
11 Jens Beckert, 'Markets from Meaning: Quality Uncertainty and the Intersubjective Construction of Value', *Cambridge Journal of Economics*, vol.44, 2020, pp 285–301, p.288.
12 See also Kathryn Brown, 'Art Markets, Epistemic Authority, and the Institutional Curation of Knowledge', *Cultural Studies*, vol.37, no.4, 2023, pp 626–46.
13 Carol Vogel, 'Phillips de Pury Wants to Make a Big Splash', *The New York Times*, 27 May 2010, https://www.nytimes.com/2010/05/28/arts/design/28vogel.html?ref=arts. Accessed 2 August 2023.
14 Interview with the author, 27 November 2023.
15 See an interview with Vincent Darré about the Artcurial sale on the auction house's website, https://www.artcurial.com/en/news/artcurial-reveals-name-interior-designer-who-will-take-care-installation-ritz-exhibition-paris. Accessed 2 August 2023; Rachael Sigee, 'Superhero, Indie Darling and Guest Curator: Robert Pattinson's Picks', Sotheby's, 16 September 2022, https://www.sothebys.com/en/articles/superhero-indie-darling-and-guest-curator-robert-pattinsons-picks. Accessed 2 August 2023.
16 Edward Helmore, 'Modigliani nude fetches $157.2m at Sotheby's – setting

auction house record', *The Guardian*, 15 May 2018, https://www.theguardian.com/artanddesign/2018/may/14/modigliani-nude-auction-sothebys-new-york-record. Accessed 11 December 2023.

17 Georgina Adam, 'Show and Sell: The Added Value of a Museum Exhibition', *The Art Newspaper*, 12 June 2018, https://www.theartnewspaper.com/2018/06/12/show-and-sell-the-added-value-of-a-museum-exhibition. Accessed 1 August 2023.

18 Christopher Knight, 'Baltimore Museum of Art uses COVID as Cover to Sell a Warhol. Floodgates Open', *LA Times*, 19 October 2020, https://www.latimes.com/entertainment-arts/story/2020-10-19/baltimore-museum-art-auction-andy-warhol-last-supper. Accessed 1 August 2023.

19 Nizan Shaked, *Museums and Wealth: The Politics of Contemporary Art* (London: Bloomsbury, 2022), p.54.

20 For an overview see Renée Grimaud, *50 ans d'expositions au Grand Palais* (Paris: Réunion des musées nationaux, 2009).

21 See the summary report on the website of the Grand Palais, https://www.grandpalais.fr/en/article/auction-sale-yves-saint-laurent-pierre-berge-collection-february-21-25-2009. Accessed 1 August 2023.

22 See the description on Villa Grisebach's webpage, https://www.grisebach.com/en/auction-house/philosophy-history.html. Accessed 1 August 2023.

23 Edwin Heathcote, 'Auction houses become sophisticated in their architecture', *The Financial Times*, 14 November 2014, https://www.ft.com/content/3581aff8-68ca-11e4-9eeb-00144feabdc0. Accessed 1 August 2023.

24 Moon So-Young and Yoo Joo-Hyun, 'Young Collectors, New Outlets Help Continued Growth of Korea's Art Market', *Korea JoongAng Daily*, 10 March 2022, https://koreajoongangdaily.joins.com/2022/03/10/culture/artsDesign/department-stores-korean-art-art-market/20220310163230581.html. Accessed 2 August 2023; Joon Bae Kim, 'Korea's Shinsegae Department Store Seeks Direct Entry Into the Auction Market', *Auction Daily*, 9 February 2023, https://auctiondaily.com/news/koreas-shinsegae-department-store-seeks-direct-entry-into-the-auction-market/. Accessed 2 August 2023.

25 Studio MDA, 'Phillips New York Headquarters', Summer 2021, https://studiomda.com/phillips-headquarters. Accessed 2 August 2023.

26 ibid.

27 Guardian Art Center website, https://www.cguardianart.com/index.php?webLg=en_us. Accessed 2 August 2023.

28 ibid.

29 Kejia Wu, *A Modern History of China's Art Market* (Abingdon: Routledge, 2023), pp 68–9.

30 Noah Horowitz, *The Art of the Deal. Contemporary Art in a Global Financial Market* (Princeton: Princeton University Press, 2014); Christl Baur, 'Ars Electronica and the Media Art Economy', *Journal of Visual Art Practice*, vol.19, no.3, 2020, pp 241–53.

31 For further details see Christie's, 'Is artificial intelligence set to become art's next medium?', 12 December 2018, https://www.christies.com/features/A-collaboration-between-two-artists-one-human-one-a-machine-9332-1.aspx?sc_lang=en. Accessed 2 August 2023.

32 Christie's, 'Marina Abramović's *The Life* – The World's First Mixed Reality Performance Artwork', https://www.christies.com/features/Marina-Abramovic-The-Life-10193-3.aspx?sc_lang=en#FID-10193. Accessed 16 February 2023.

33 Christie's, 'Beeple's opus', https://www.christies.com/en/stories/monumental-collage-by-beeple-is-first-purely-digital-artwork-nft-to-come-to-auction-0463a2c0f3174b17997fba8a1fe4c865. Accessed 16 February 2023.

34 See Christie's 3.0 website, https://nft.christies.com/. Accessed 16 February 2023.

## 5: Ethics and Deregulation

1 Aeron Davis, 'Defining speculative value in the age of financialized capitalism', *The Sociological Review*, vol.66, no.1, 2018, pp 3–19.

2 ibid., p.8.

3 Sotheby's, 'Pablo Picasso: Biography', https://www.sothebys.com/en/artists/pablo-picasso. Accessed 3 August 2023.

4 See, for example, Max Haiven, *Art After Money After Art: Creative Strategies Against Financialization* (London: Pluto Press, 2018), p.15.

5 Jens Beckert and Jörg Rössel, 'The Price of Art: Uncertainty and Reputation in the Art Field', *European Societies*, vol.15, no.2, 2013, pp 178–95, p.191.

6 Patricia A. Banks, 'The Rise of Africa in the Contemporary Auction Market: Myth or Reality', *Poetics*, vol.71, 2018, pp 7–17, p.15.

7 Adeyemi, *Contemporary Art from Nigeria in the Global Markets.*

8 Nate Freeman, 'The Swift, Cruel, Incredible Rise of Amoako Boafo: How Feverish Selling and Infighting Built the Buzziest Artist of 2020', *artnet news*, 28 September 2020, https://news.artnet.com/art-world/amoako-boafo-1910883. Accessed 22 August 2023.

9 ibid.

10 Christie's, 'The Last da Vinci', 12 November 2017, https://www.christies.com/features/The-last-da-Vinci-Salvator-Mundi-8598-3.aspx. Accessed 3 August 2023.

11 Christie's, 'The Life and Times of Stan', 2020, https://www.christies.com/features/The-life-of-STAN-a-T-rex-excavated-in-1992-10872-7.aspx. Accessed 3 August 2023.

12 See the case description on the webpage of the Commission for Looted Art in Europe, https://www.lootedartcommission.com/dortheum-case. Accessed 3 August 2023.

13 For further detail see Neumeister's page on provenance research, https://www.neumeister.com/en/service/provenienzforschung-restitution/. Accessed 4 August 2023.

14 Sarah Cascone, 'Old Master Painting Pulled from Auction After French Government Inquiry', *artnet*, 13 April 2016, https://news.artnet.com/art-world/bartholomeus-van-der-helst-auction-cancelled-472490. Accessed 15 February 2024.

15 Catherine Hickley, 'Nazi-looted Old Master painting withdrawn from Austrian auction at France's request', *The Art Newspaper*, 13 April 2016, https://www.theartnewspaper.com/2016/04/13/nazi-looted-old-master-painting-withdrawn-from-austrian-auction-at-frances-request. Accessed 24 August 2023.

16 Nina Siegal, 'Owner Withdraws Nazi-Looted Painting from Auction in Austria', *The New York Times*, 26 April 2017, https://www.nytimes.com/2017/04/26/arts/design/owner-withdraws-nazi-looted-painting-from-auction-in-austria.html. Accessed 4 August 2023.

17 See Emmanual Akinwotu, 'Nigerian Scholar Calls for Halt to Auction of Sacred Igbo Artworks', *The Guardian*, 21 June 2020, https://www.theguardian.com/world/2020/jun/21/nigeria-igbo-sacred-artworks-sculpture-christies-paris. Accessed 4 August 2023.

18 Bénédicte Savoy, *Africa's Struggle for its Art: History of a Postcolonial Defeat*, translated by Susanne Meyer-Abich (Princeton: Princeton University Press, 2022), p.100.

19 For a discussion of 'bidding rings' see Heath, *The Dynamics of Auction*, p.118.

20 For further discussion see Anna Bolz, *A Regulatory Framework for the Art Market: Authenticity, Forgeries and the Role of Art Experts* (Cham: Springer, 2023), p.14.

21 ibid.

22 ibid., p.5.

23 Anja Shortland and Andrew Shortland, 'Governance Under the Shadow of the Law: Trading High Value Fine Art', *Public Choice*, vol.184, 2020, pp 157–74, p.158.

24 ibid.

25 ibid., p.171. The authors also note that the most expensive auction houses are located in jurisdictions with strong legal frameworks that protect buyers and sellers.

26 See, for example, Georgina Adam and Charlotte Burns, 'Auction guarantees are dividing the art trade', *The Art Newspaper*, 1 March 2011, https://www.theartnewspaper.com/2011/03/01/auction-guarantees-are-dividing-the-art-trade. Accessed 23 November 2023.

27 Georgina Adam, *The Dark Side of the Boom: The Excesses of the Art Market in the 21st Century* (London: Lund Humphries, 2017), p.81.

28 Judd Tully, 'Hedge to Hedge: A secondary market for third-party auction guarantees is on the rise', *The Art Newspaper*, 5 May 2023, https://www.theartnewspaper.com/2023/05/05/hedge-to-hedge-a-secondary-market-for-third-party-auction-guarantees-is-on-the-rise. Accessed 23 November 2023.

29 'The Intelligence Report: Mid-Year Review', *artnet*, August 2023, p.45, https://media.artnet.com/image/upload/v1691415983/2023/08/introducing-the-artnet-intelligence-report-mid-year-review-2023_oqhquy.pdf. Accessed 10 August 2023.

30 For a summary of the changes see Joseph A. Patella and Rachel E. Hudgins, 'New York City Lifts Rules Governing Auctions', *National Law Review*, 8 June 2022, https://www.natlawreview.com/article/new-york-city-lifts-rules-governing-auctions. Accessed 8 August 2023.

### Conclusion

1 Christie's, 'A Message from Guillaume Cerutti, Christie's Chief Executive Officer', January 2024, https://m1.emails.christies.com/nl/jsp/m.jsp?c=%40xAHDBFV2CNloeZ52FNxZloqhBRGCWyQvzGq%2FX2TKkpo%3D&COSID=42338629&cid=DM502597&bid=388806100. Accessed 19 January 2024.

2 ibid.

3 Interview with the author, 27 November 2023.

# Further Reading


Adam, Georgina, *The Dark Side of the Boom, The Excesses of the Art Market in the 21st Century* (Lund Humphries, London, 2017)

Adeyemi, Jonathan, *Contemporary Art from Nigeria in the Global Markets, Trending in the Margins* (Palgrave Macmillan, Cham, Switzerland, 2022)

Appadurai, Arjun (ed.), *The Social Life of Things, Commodities in Cultural Perspective* (Cambridge University Press, Cambridge, 1986)

Archer, Anita, 'Materializing Markets, The Agency of Auctions in Emergent Art Genres in the Global South', *Arts*, vol.9, no.106 (2020), pp 1–14

Becker, Howard S., *Art Worlds*, 2nd edition (University of California Press, Berkeley, 2008)

Beckert, Jens and Aspers, Patrik (eds), *The Worth of Goods, Valuation and Pricing in the Economy* (Oxford University Press, Oxford, 2011)

Boll, Dirk (ed.), *Auctioneers Who Made Art History* (Hatje Cantz, Berlin, 2020)

Boltanski, Luc and Esquerre, Arnaud, *Enrichment, A Critique of Commodities*, translated by Catherine Porter (Polity, Cambridge, 2020)

Bolz, Anna, *A Regulatory Framework for the Art Market, Authenticity, Forgeries and the Role of Art Experts* (Springer, Cham, Switzerland, 2023)

Brown, Kathryn, 'Disappearing Acts, Fictitious Capital, Aesthetic Atheism, and the Artworld', *Journal of Visual Art Practice*, vol.19, no.3 (2020), pp 225–40

Brown, Kathryn, 'Screen Culture, Online Auctions, and Art Market Spectacle', *Visual Studies*, vol.38, nos 3–4 (2023), pp 377–88

Brown, Kathryn, 'Art Markets, Epistemic Authority, and the Institutional Curation of Knowledge', *Cultural Studies*, vol.37, no.4 (2023), pp 626–46

Buchholz, Larissa, *The Global Rules of Art* (Princeton University Press, Princeton, 2022)

Cassady Jr, Ralph, *Auctions and Auctioneering* (University of California Press, Berkeley, 2021)

Degen, Natasha (ed.), *The Art Market* (Whitechapel Gallery, London, and MIT Press, Massachusetts, 2013)

Ekelund Jr, Robert B., Jackson, John D. and Tollison, Robert D., *The Economics of American Art, Issues, Artists, and Market Institutions* (Oxford University Press, Oxford, 2017)

Findlay, Michael, *The Value of Art, Money, Power, Beauty*, 2nd edition (Prestel, Munich, 2022)

Heath, Christian, *The Dynamics of Auction, Social Interaction and the Sale of Fine Art and Antiquities* (Cambridge University Press, Cambridge, 2014)

Hook, Philip, *Rogues' Gallery, A History of Art and its Dealers* (Profile Books, London, 2017)

Huda, Shireen, *Pedigree and Panache, A History of the Art Auction in Australia* (Australian National University, Canberra, 2008)

Learmount, Brian, *A History of the Auction from 500 BC to the Present Day* (The Book Guild Ltd, Market Harborough, 2021)

Milano, Ronit, 'Moralizing the Art Market, A Socioeconomic Perspective on Art Auctions on the Floor and Online', *Journal for Art Market Studies*, vol.1 (2019), pp 1–18

Milgrom, Paul R. and Weber, Robert J., 'A Theory of Auctions and Competitive Bidding', *Econometrica*, vol.50, no.5 (1982), pp 1089–122

Montias, John Michael, *Art at Auction in 17th Century Amsterdam* (Amsterdam University Press, Amsterdam, 2002)

Muensterberger, Werner, *Collecting, An Unruly Passion, Psychological Perspectives* (Princeton University Press, Princeton, 1994)

Ott, John, 'How New York Stole the Luxury Art Market, Blockbuster Auctions and Bourgeois Identity in Gilded Age America', *Winterthur Portfolio*, vol.42, nos 2–3 (2008), pp 133–58

Quemin, Alain, *Le Monde des galeries, Art contemporain, structure du marché et internationalisation* (CNRS Editions, Paris, 2021)

Salemink, O., Siegel Corrêa, A., Sejrup, J., and Nielsen, V. (eds), *Global Art in Local Artworlds, Changing Hierarchies of Value* (Routledge, Abingdon, 2023)

Shaked, Nizan, *Museums and Wealth, The Politics of Contemporary Art* (Bloomsbury, London, 2022)

Smith, Charles W., *Auctions, The Social Construction of Value* (University of California Press, Berkeley, 1990)

Sooudi, Olga Kanzaki, 'Making Mumbai's Emerging Art World through Makeshift Practices', *Journal of South Asian Studies*, vol.39, no.1 (2016), pp 149–66

Sreberny-Mohammadi, Leili, 'The Emergence of an Auction Category, Iranian Art at Christie's Dubai, 2006–2016', *Arts*, vol.10, no.35 (2021)

Thaler, Richard H., 'Anomalies, The Winner's Curse', *Journal of Economic Perspectives*, vol.2, no.1 (1988), pp 191–202

Veblen, Thorstein, *The Theory of the Leisure Class, An Economic Study of Institutions* (Oxford University Press, Oxford, 2009)

Velthuis, Olav, *Talking Prices, Symbolic Meanings of Prices on the Market for Contemporary Art* (Princeton University Press, Princeton, 2005)

Velthuis, Olav and Baia Curioni, Stefano (eds), *Cosmopolitan Canvases, The Globalization of Markets for Contemporary Art* (Oxford University Press, Oxford, 2015)

Vickrey, William, 'Counterspeculation, Auctions, and Competitive Sealed Tenders', *The Journal of Finance*, vol.16, no.1 (1961), pp 8–37

Wall, Cynthia, 'The English Auction, Narratives of Dismantlings', *Eighteenth-Century Studies*, vol.31, no.1 (1997), pp 1–25

Wu, Kejia, *A Modern History of China's Art Market* (Routledge, Abingdon, 2023)

Zheng, Zhen, *The Legal System of Art Auctions in China* (Springer, Singapore, 2022)

# Index

Note: page numbers followed by n refer to notes.